Financialisation in the Automotive Industry

Where presidents or members of affluent families were previously seen, it is increasingly the case that car manufacturers are owned by banks and investment funds which have taken control of the entire economic life of these firms. This has significant impact on the terms of employment and layoffs, wages and precarious work, growing inequalities in income strata, compensation levels for executives, and the implementation of short-termist strategies across business operations.

This book explores this increasing financialisation – the predominance of the financial sector over the productive sector – in the automotive industry. In particular it is shown that the financial operations of these companies through leasing, insurance, loans and other financial instruments is now much more profitable than the manufacturing aspects of the business, which was originally the raison d'être for these firms. The chapters demonstrate how there are great demands to increase the return to shareholders as a main concern, despite other metrics and/or other stakeholders. The work studies the impact of financialisation at the world's five largest automakers which together represent almost 50% of car production, providing an exploratory analysis of profitability, shareholder composition, compensation to executives, workers' salaries, dividend payments to shareholders and employment.

Encouraging debate on contemporary economy, this book marks a significant addition to the literature on financialisation, contemporary forms of capitalism, labour and economic sociology more broadly.

Marcelo José do Carmo has a PhD in Production Engineering at the Federal University of São Carlos, São Paulo, Brazil.

Mário Sacomano Neto is Associated Professor of Organizational Theory at the Federal University of Sao Carlos, UFSCar, Brazil.

Julio Cesar Donadone is currently Full Professor at the Federal University of São Carlos, Brazil, and coordinator of the Center of Studies on Economic Sociology and Finance NESEFI -UFSCar.

Routledge Frontiers of Political Economy

China's Belt and Road Initiative
The Impact on Sub-regional Southeast Asia
Edited by Christian Ploberger, Soavapa Ngampamuan and Tao Song

Capital and Capitalism
Old Myths, New Futures
Rogene A. Buchholz

Economic Change and Wellbeing
The True Cost of Creative Destruction and Globalization
Fabio D'Orlando, Francesco Ferrante and Albertina Oliverio

Capitalism, Development and Empowerment of Labour
A Heterodox Political Economy
Hartmut Elsenhans

Financialisation in the Automotive Industry
Capital and Labour in Contemporary Society
Marcelo José do Carmo, Mário Sacomano Neto and Julio Cesar Donadone

Political Economy of Financialization in the United States
A Historical-Institutional Balance-Sheet Approach
Kurt Mettenheim

For more information about this series, please visit: www.routledge.com/Routledge-Frontiers-of-Political-Economy/book-series/SE0345

Financialisation in the Automotive Industry

Capital and Labour in Contemporary Society

Marcelo José do Carmo, Mário Sacomano Neto and Julio Cesar Donadone

Translation by **Jane Godwin Coury**

Routledge
Taylor & Francis Group

LONDON AND NEW YORK

First published 2022
by Routledge
2 Park Square, Milton Park, Abingdon, Oxon OX14 4RN

and by Routledge
605 Third Avenue, New York, NY 10158

Routledge is an imprint of the Taylor & Francis Group, an informa business

© 2022 Marcelo José do Carmo, Mário Sacomano Neto
and Julio Cesar Donadone

The right of Marcelo José do Carmo, Mário Sacomano Neto and
Julio Cesar Donadone to be identified as authors of this work has been
asserted by them in accordance with sections 77 and 78 of the Copyright,
Designs and Patents Act 1988.

British Library Cataloguing-in-Publication Data
A catalogue record for this book is available from the British Library

Library of Congress Cataloging-in-Publication Data
Names: Do Carmo, Marcelo José, 1973– author. |
Sacomano Neto, Mário, author. | Donadone, Julio Cesar, author.
Title: Financialisation in the automotive industry : capital and
labour in contemporary society / Marcelo José do Carmo,
Mário Sacomano Neto and Julio Cesar Donadone.
Description: 1 Edition. | New York, NY : Routledge, 2022. |
Series: Routledge frontiers of political economy |
Includes bibliographical references and index.
Identifiers: LCCN 2021014379 (print) | LCCN 2021014380 (ebook)
Subjects: LCSH: Automobile industry and trade–Finance. |
Financialization. | Economic policy. | Manpower planning. |
Economics–Sociological aspects.
Classification: LCC HD9710.A2 D6 2022 (print) |
LCC HD9710.A2 (ebook) | DDC 338.4/76292220681–dc23
LC record available at https://lccn.loc.gov/2021014379
LC ebook record available at https://lccn.loc.gov/2021014380

ISBN: 978-0-367-75139-5 (hbk)
ISBN: 978-0-367-75140-1 (pbk)
ISBN: 978-1-003-16114-1 (ebk)

DOI: 10.4324/9781003161141

Typeset in Times New Roman
by Newgen Publishing UK

Contents

Figures

Tables

About the authors

Marcelo José do Carmo has a PhD in Production Engineering at the Federal University of São Carlos, São Paulo, Brazil (2020). He has a Bachelor in Social Sciences, with a concentration in Political Science, from the Federal University of São Carlos (1999) and a Master's in Production Engineering (2017) from the same institution. He was visiting researcher at PMO Alliance Manchester Business School (UK), under the supervision of Prof. Dr Ismail Erturk (2020). His interests are about politics, sociology and economy, particularly economic sociology, financialisation, organisations, shareholders, executives, employees, salaries and employment.

Mário Sacomano Neto is Associated Professor of Organizational Theory at Federal University of Sao Carlos, UFSCar, Brazil. He has a Bachelor in Business and Management from Pontifical Catholic University, a PhD in Industrial Engineering from Federal University of São Carlos and a Master's in Industrial Engineering from the University of São Paulo (USP). He was Visiting Scholar at the University of California, Berkeley, under supervision of Neil Fligstein (Department of Sociology) and Visiting Scholar at the University of Chicago (USA) under the supervision of Professor Gary Herrigel and John Padgett (Political Science Department). His current research project is funded by the Brazilian Research National Agency.

Julio Cesar Donadone is currently Full Professor at the Federal University of São Carlos, Brazil, and coordinator of the Center of Studies on Economic Sociology and Finance NESEFI -UFSCar. He was a visiting researcher at the University of California, Berkeley, USA (1998 and 2018) and EHESS – École des Hautes Études en Sciences Sociales – Paris, France (2005). He has experience in sociology, with emphasis on economic sociology, working mainly on the following topics: intermediaries, financialisation and dynamics of fields.

Foreword

by Ismail Ertürk

Since the 2007 Global Financial Crisis (GFC) the financialisation studies have been primarily about the socioeconomic consequences of the financial sector that caused one of the biggest crises in the history of capitalism comparable to the Wall Street Crash of 1929. Too-big-to-fail banks, complex global interconnectedness of financial institutions and financial markets, high levels of indebtedness of governments, corporates, and households have been studied by an expanding number of social science disciplines from anthropology to economic history, from literary studies to urban studies. What this book reminds us is the origins of the financialisation studies: financialisation of giant manufacturing firms. Of course the transformation of finance capital into a self-referential speculative socioeconomic system detached from the productive dynamics of the economy and corroding the possibilities of social cohesion between productive capital and high-wage labour justifies the critical scholarly attention it has received since the GFC. But the zombie capitalist economy since the GFC and after trillions of dollars of quantitative easing by the central banks in capitalism's centre necessitates a reminder about the socioeconomic consequences of non-financial firms' financialisation and also about the importance of empirical work on non-financial firms' accounting and financial data where financialised relationship between labour and capital, and between management and institutional shareholders are represented. What can be more ironic than hearing this fact from the CEO of the world's largest institutional investor, BlackRock. In 2015 Larry Fink wrote an open letter to the boards of the S&P 500 companies in the United States criticising their financialised behaviour:

> corporate leaders have responded with actions that can deliver immediate returns to shareholders, such as buybacks or divided increases, while under-investing in innovation, skilled workforces

or essential capital expenditures necessary to sustain long-term growth.

(Fink, 2015)

In this letter Fink was referring to the failure of quantitative easing in creating private investment-led growth in the U.S. He was not alone in blaming the financialised behaviour of firms for a capitalism where rich corporations with spectacular stock market valuations coexist with poor societies and governments with big fiscal deficits. The President of Dallas Federal Reserve, Richard Fisher (2013), the chief economist of the Bank of England, Andrew Haldane (2015), and the OECD (2015) economists, too, agreed with Fink and identified shareholder-value driven firms as responsible for the failure of unprecedented central bank monetary policy since the GFC.

Stock markets currently reward companies that favour dividends and buybacks and punish those that undertake more investment … which creates higher hurdle rates for investment in the current uncertain environment.

(OECD, 2015, p.31)

What the CEO of Blackrock, central bankers and OECD draw attention to at the macroeconomic level this book demonstrates through case studies in car industry globally – an industry that is vital in many ways for their own national economies as well as for the global economy. Volkswagen, Toyota, Hyundai, Ford and General Motors are major contributors to the economic fabric in their respective countries.

Through these case studies we observe at the micro level how the logic of financialisation operates in non-financial giant corporations and how this corrodes a productive economy with the consequences of the enrichment of top management, whose remuneration is linked to stock market valuations, and the impoverishment of wage labour and fixed capital formation in national economies. As such this book contributes in a timely manner to the financialisation studies by allowing us to reflect on how an economic recovery after the Covid-19 crisis is likely to be impeded if share buybacks, higher dividends, equity linked remuneration of executives are preferred to investments and higher wages.

As well as providing an empirical analysis of financialisation at the world's leading car companies the book also contextualises these case studies of financialisation within the financialisation literature and its contribution to economic sociology. A comprehensive literature review of financialisation of non-financial firms and the earlier academic work on the financialisation of car companies precedes the empirical case studies.

Ismail Ertürk
Senior Lecturer in Banking
Alliance Manchester Business School
The University of Manchester, UK

References

Fink, L. (14 April 2015) BlackRock CEO Larry Fink tells the world's biggest business leaders to stop worrying about short-term results. *Business Insider*. Available from: www.businessinsider.com/larry-fink-letter-to-ceos-2015-4?IR=T. Accessed on 10 July 2015.

Fisher, R. W. (2013) Horseshift! (With Reference to Gordian Knots). Remarks before the National Association of State Retirement Administrators 59th Annual Conference, 5 August 2013. Available from: www.dallasfed.org/news/speeches/fisher/2013/fs130805.cfm Accessed 17 August 2014.

Haldane, A. (22 May 2015) Who owns a company? Speech delivered at University of Edinburgh Corporate Finance Conference. Available from: www.bankofengland.co.uk/speech/2015/who-owns-a-company Accessed 20 July 2015.

OECD (2015) *OECD Business and Finance Outlook 2015*. OECD Publishing, Paris.

Acknowledgements

The authors would like to thank the Coordination for the Improvement of Higher Education Personnel (CAPES) for the financial support, without which it would not have been possible to develop this research.

1 Introduction

Introduction

The automotive sector is going through a growing financialisation process, which has been considered as the preference for capital appreciation through financial activities rather than productive activities. In this process, there is a tendency for capital to increase in value through activities that do not need to go through production or that take place after production itself. Moreover, the automotive sector has become the object of acquisitions and increased participation by banks, investment funds and financial institutions in their property rights. Thus, there is enormous pressure from top executives and shareholders for an ever-greater return on investments.

This propensity to maximise shareholder value has become recurring practice for automakers, where the search for profit reaches 12%, 15% return on capital employed annually, which can only be achieved through financial activities and not in the mature and cyclical automotive products market, historically a sector of poor performance and narrow profit margins, yielding around 5 to 7% per year. Automakers have achieved the profitability required by shareholders and controllers only through the intensification of financial activities such as leasing, financing and other "products" launched by their subsidiaries.

To what extent is financialisation important in people's lives?

The main effects of the financialisation process in industrial and productive sectors are related to the increasing importance of the financial pole in the business as a whole. Shareholder expectations become the number one concern for companies and the idea that all stakeholders have the same weight is only in the narrative and rhetoric field, implying that it is more due to advertising than a concrete reality. An example is employment in the automotive sector, mainly at North American automakers, as we will see in the cases of Ford and General Motors, in

DOI: 10.4324/9781003161141-1

which there has been a movement of intense destruction of jobs over the last three decades. Meanwhile, dividend payments to shareholders have been constant and growing, in direct opposition to the creation of vacancies. In other words, the priority is to create value for shareholders and not for all stakeholders who, in the case of workers, have suffered thousands of layoffs and factory closures in recent years.

The differences in earnings between company managers and employees' wages are widening, creating a gap between the wage layers, increasing economic inequality in society and flattening wages in an industry that has always been considered the dream of every worker.

To make this work feasible, a multi-case study was used to select the five largest automotive companies in the world, in terms of production volume, according to data from the International Organisation of Automobile Manufacturers, OICA (2015a). The top five automakers in 2014 were Toyota, Volkswagen, GM, Hyundai and Ford and they accounted for around 50% of world production. To analyse financialisation, seven indicators that comprise this process were investigated, such as the proportion of profit from finance compared to the profit obtained from production, shareholding composition of companies, equity acquisitions, the origin of company directors and dividend payments to shareholders, in addition to compensation to executives, workers' salaries and employment.

The central idea is that financialisation is the economic characteristic that has most marked contemporary capitalism, changing the relationship between capital and labour worldwide, in favour of a reduced social layer of shareholders. It was hoped, with this work, to contribute to the research agenda of economic sociology, a current of thought that defends the unification of various social sciences in the explanation of economic phenomena. Thus, we would be able to learn more about the financialisation process in the automotive sector, one of the largest and most important industrial sectors in the economy.

Theoretical conceptions on financialisation

The process of financialisation of production can be characterised by the growing acquisition of stock rights that banks, pension funds, investment funds, mutual funds and insurance companies now hold from manufacturing companies. It can also be characterised by the institution of a new ideology, that of maximising shareholder value and transforming a strategy based on retaining and reinvesting to another one of decreasing and distributing resources to shareholders (Lazonick and O'Sullivan, 2000, p. 13). Over the past few decades, there has been a change in significance from the real sector to the financial sector (Dunhaupt, 2010), in addition to the increased importance of shareholder appreciation in the short term (Hardie, 2008) and the power of CEOs to increase from the 1980s (Boyer, 2005).

Neil Fligstein (1990) studied the main stages that corporate control in capitalism went through since his family time, moving from the individual company to the diversified group focusing on manufacturing and management, later being gradually replaced by the vision of marketing and sales, to then be replaced by the current phase, whose leaders participating in the world of finance had a preponderance in corporate control. Fligstein analyses the types of control conception that, for him, are the result of interactions between states, markets and companies, acting in a large organisational field, in which companies, consumers, suppliers, and competitors orbit, among others (Donadone and Matsuda, 2015).

Michael Useem (1996) analysed the changes that occurred in the functioning of company management and the modification of managers' power, passing this power to the control of the shareholders. In his famous book: *Investor Capitalism*, he says that due to the dispersion of shareholders, power shifted from the owner of the company to professional managers who had a high degree of autonomy and almost no external control to the firm, nor supervision. These managers dominated until the 1980s when a struggle for control of companies began to take place through the boards of directors, which brought together "dissatisfied shareholders and disappointed directors". This struggle wound the death of the hitherto unquestioned sovereignty of managers and transferred effective power to shareholders, hence the mentality of maximising shareholder value, millionaire compensation to executives and short-term appreciation of the business was developed (Useem, 1996, p.15).

Some authors argue that a new financial capitalism is in full force, at least in the United States, with the crisis of managerialism in post-industrialism and a transition from manufacturing to services. Besides, the borders that involve finance as an industry became much more "porous" in the 1990s and 2000s, "with many types of firms earning much of their profits through financial activities even though they are considered non-financial companies, as is the case of GE, GM and Enron" (Davis, 2009, pp.236–239).

This is the reality of large industrial groups, in which the profitability of financial capital far exceeds the profitability and profits of production (Chesnais, 1996; Piketty, 2014; Godechot, 2015). François Chesnais (1996) studied the globalisation of capital and concluded that "for large groups in the manufacturing or services sector, the close inter-mingling between the productive and financial dimensions of the globalisation of capital today represents an element inherent to their daily functioning" (Chesnais, 1996, p.275). According to the French author, industrial groups are financial groups with an industrial predominance. He says that industrial groups have diversified towards finance and that globalisation has forced them to accentuate their role as financial centres. Industrial groups are active agents of financial globalisation, as he asserted in his classic 1996 book. In this book, he debates the inter-penetration between industry and finance, a process that characterised the end of the 19th century, exposed in texts by Rudolf Hilferding, in addition to other Marxists, such as Lenin, who discussed the "merger" between industrial capital and banking capital, resulting in financial capital (Chesnais, 1996, p.290).

Claude Serfati (1999) studied the participation of industrial groups in the financialisation of the economy, and in this study, he defines a group as a holding company that centralises assets, "qualified as 'productive' and 'financial' and that are profit generators". He hypothesises that "the cleavages between these two forms of valuation, often considered to be 'polar', are now less clearly demarcated than is thought" (Serfati, 1999, p.142).

For Gerald Epstein (2002) "financialisation refers to the increasing importance of financial markets, financial objectives, financial institutions, and financial elites in the operation of the economy and in the management of these institutions, both at the national and inter-national levels (Epstein, 2002, p.3). Robert Guttmann (1999) states that Marx, in book III of *Capital*, already made the distinction between two forms of financial capital:

> medium- or long-term loans, with interest, and what he (Marx) calls 'capital fictitious' [...] this would cover credits involving future cash commitments (bonds), the value of which is determined solely by the capitalisation of the expected return, without a direct coun-terpart in productive capital.
>
> (Guttmann, 1999, p.77)

It would therefore be the transformation from productive capitalism to financial capitalism (Martins, 2014, p.116). Davis and Kim (2015) begin one of their most recent works by stating that "financialisation refers to the increasing importance of finance, financial markets and financial institutions in the functioning of the economy" (Davis and Kim, 2015).

Together, we can infer a minimum of agreement in the basic conception: financialisation would be the transformation of industrial capitalism, as the main source of capital appreciation for financial capitalism (Zilbovicius and Dias, 2006), and the advance of fictitious capital, as a product of considerable autonomy of circulation over production (Mollo, 2011, p.2).

When we look at studies on economic inequality, many analysts of contemporary capitalism point to the widening of trends in the profitability of financial capital well above the profitability of productive capital and income from production.

One of them, Thomas Piketty, in his book: *Capital in the 21st Century*, states that the equation r > g, (rent bigger than growth, that is, the annual rate of return on capital is higher than the annual growth rate of population, production and income from work), presents itself as an inexorable reality of the current economic moment of humanity and is leading society to an accumulation of capital in few hands and to an economic inequality only known in the 1910s in Europe of the Belle Époque (Piketty, 2014, p.33).

> According to this idea
> since the 1970s and 1980s, there has been a strong movement towards financialisation of the economy and the structure of assets. That is, the volume of financial assets and liabilities held by the different sectors (families, firms, government) has expanded even more intensely than the net value of assets.
>
> (Piketty, 2014, p.191)

And this movement "reflects the unprecedented evolution of cross-shareholdings between financial and non-financial companies in the same country [...] as well as cross-shareholdings between countries" (Piketty, 2014, p.191).

This situation leads to the development of a society supposedly of a meritocratic type, where there is the creation of super-executives, whose income from work is seen as more than was seen previously when income from inheritance predominated. For super-executives and those in the salary range responsible for less than 1% of the population, this situation in the social hierarchy is defended as positive and normal (Piketty, 2014, p.259). Super-executives, mostly found in the United States (Piketty, 2014, p.283) populate the upper-income bracket, 0.1%, and are responsible for the bulk of the participation in the highest salaries. Although they have a share of almost 10% of GDP, finance executives share about 20% of high salaries. And "80% of the highest incomes do not come from finance, but the increase in these American incomes is explained, first of all, by the explosion in the remuneration of top executives of large companies, whether they are in the financial sector or not" (Piketty, 2014, p.295).

Another French author, Olivier Godechot, a researcher at the Max Planck Institute of Sciences, published a study on the impact of the various dimensions of financialisation on the increase in economic inequality at a global level and concluded that financialisation is marketing, – Marketisation!, through which the market creates new niches that are occupied by financial intermediaries that can earn extraordinary gains, increasing the gap between the salary ranges and allowing a concentration of income from work in the upper hundredth bracket, increasing inequality (Godechot, 2015).

According to Godechot, the concept of financialisation is multidimensional, which may refer to the financial sector as a whole and to the increase in its weight in the economy as a whole, as well as to the non-financial sector, whether families or firms. He argues that financialisation has been seen exclusively as an attempt to transform non-financial firms into financialised companies from the perspective of maximising shareholder value. While this is true, the result of his study demonstrates that the most profound impact on economic inequality over the past forty years is the creation of a financial market, whereby "the organisation of work allows some actors to capture some of the key assets" that is, there is the emergence of a market whose fruit is "the link between finance and inequality [that] is mainly due to the apparition of a rent on the financial markets and its appropriation by a minority" (Godechot, 2015, p.20), thus increasing economic inequality.

Besides the concrete and visible aspect of financialisation, the semiotic, symbolic, cultural aspects of the narratives of this phenomenon have also been studied by authors such as Julie Froud, Sukhdev Johal and Karel Williams. They claim that a process of legitimation based on the narratives told by the leaders seeks to support the physical process of financialisation. The arguments about correcting this or that way of managing the company generally have nothing to do with the performance itself. They are only narratives to justify decisions within companies (Froud et al., 2006). The authors emphasised the need to promote new research for a better understanding of the financial framework of society since several changes have occurred and the previous analysis methods, based on factories, processes and products, would already be obsolete (Froud et al., 2002).

Along the same lines, Mariana Mazzucato (2014) seeks to unmask the myth that there would be between the public sector versus the private sector in her book *The Entrepreneur State*. In this book, the author states that the supposed dichotomy between the state on the one hand and the market on the other is entirely false and that state and market complement each other and should thus act for the good of the whole of society. She also says that the view of the state as inert, weak, heavy and fearful does not match the empirical data observed in her research. Even in the United States, where the neoliberal and minimal state is intended, it is there that there are the largest amounts of public resources invested in science and technology on the entire planet. It is only after the state breaks the frontiers of technology and leaves uncertainty behind that the private sector seeks to participate in order to, obviously, take advantage of it as it does in any business. As she says, "venture capital does not like risks, this is just a myth" (Mazzucato, 2014, p.80).

As part of the mode of financial domination, this is the process of restructuring companies, which means that that old company, Taylorist or Fordist, whose expression was managers and focus on manufacturing, was replaced by a new dominant entity: the shareholder. Working to maximise shareholder value has become a corollary to the new mode of financial domination.

Recent research shows that financial logic greatly changes the company's existence regarding management, personnel and the general mentality of the actors. In the case study of a company in the Brazilian electric sector in São Paulo, where the authors analysed the construction of careers at different times of the company's existence, before and after privatisation, one of the conclusions was that "pressure from new owners has consequences in the organisational design and in the composition of the company's power" (Donadone and Matsuda, 2015, p.420).

In her book *Liquidated* (2009), the American anthropologist Karen Ho addressed the issue of jobs under the aegis of financialisation in her Wall Street ethnography. According to her, investment bank employees have the objective of earning as much time as they can, as they always have the possibility of being fired. It would be what she calls a liquid, fluid age, without many established roots or lasting commitments. Moreover, this fluidity in relations has been growing rapidly.

In the Brazilian retail sector, the study by Saltorato et al. (2014) shed light on the financialisation process that has been occurring at a fast pace and its organisational impacts and commercial objectives. The authors analysed the increasingly close connections that retail companies have maintained with financial institutions and "the intense concentration of the industry, a greater participation of foreign capital, the globalisation of business operations and the professionalisation of management, which led to a greater receptivity to financial logic by retail" (Saltorato et al., 2014, p.111). In this study, the hypothesis was raised that the commercial logic may be subordinated to the financial logic when determining management strategies. Furthermore, the authors questioned the organisational consequences that a retailer may have if he/she started to make more profits through financial activities than profits obtained by traditional retail activities (Saltorato et al., 2014, p.111). Finally, they come to the conclusion that the retailers themselves involved with other financial institutions in the launching of credit cards and exploitation of the consumer credit market believe that the proportion of their financial profits has grown faster than their profits from conventional retail activities (Saltorato et al., 2014, p.118).

Alongside increasing profitability through financial activities, one of the most important aspects of financialisation is the search for maximising shareholder value, considered by some to be the most important aspect of financialisation.

Supporting the basic premise that capital appreciation is more efficient through financial logic, the introduction of Maximising Shareholder Value (MSV) as a principle to be pursued is one of the main products of financialisation. This principle has been analysed by several researchers, much of it critically (Lazonick and O'Sullivan, 2000; Kädtler and Sperling, 2002; Jurgens et al., 2002; Moerman and Van der Laan, 2007; Ezzamel et al., 2008; Newberry and Robb, 2008; Goutas and Lane, 2009; Lazonick, 2011, 2012, 2013; Stout, 2013), but also in an uncritical and encouraging, even prescriptive way (Rappaport, 1981, 2006; Day and Fahey, 1990; Srivastava et al., 1998; Minchington and Francis, 2000; Maubossin, 2011).

According to William Lazonick and Mary O'Sullivan, one of the central points of the financialisation process is the introduction of the principle of MSV, which means the return to shareholders of their investments with a high degree of appreciation, that is, it is defended as a corollary maximising return to shareholders as a new ideology (Lazonick and O'Sullivan, 2000, p.13). The authors emphasise the transition from the concept of "retaining and reinvesting" profits to "decreasing and distributing" in the form of dividends to shareholders and compensation to executives. The previous conception, based on production, was intended to retain a good part of the earnings to be able to reinvest, and thus grow the business. This position was replaced by the assumption that profits should, in the overwhelming majority, be periodically distributed to the company's shareholders and directors, leaving the workers and other employees in the background.

In this 2000 study, Lazonick and O'Sullivan analysed the evolution of compensation to CEOs, company profits, inflation and factory wages in the United States, from 1980 to 1995. They demonstrated that the growth in compensation to CEOs had reached 499% in these 15 years. Companies' profits grew 145%, inflation 85% and wages, in last place, only grew 70% in the same period, an appreciation of less than 5% per year, seven times less than the valuation of CEOs' compensations (Lazonick and O'Sullivan, 2000, p.25).

When we talk about the proportion that executive compensation and earnings represent in total, in 1996 payments to executives consumed 54% of the total distributions, 10% were from company profits and less than 5% went to workers' wages, reaching 3% in 1998. Compensations also fell, but for a robust 35% of the total for executives (Lazonick and O'Sullivan, 2000, p.26).

The view that the principle of the MSV is universally positive is questioned by Lazonick and O'Sullivan. They claim that for shareholders and top management there were certainly many gains and advantages under the MSV rule, but that this did not translate into either economic performance for the country or general gains for society, since the US economy periodically goes into serious and deep crises and this affects the most economically vulnerable in the first place. This novelty in the MSV rule was unable to prevent crises from arising and harming large sections of the population (Lazonick and O'Sullivan, 2000, p.27).

Another author, Ismail Erturk (2015), agrees that what most characterises financialisation is the pursuit of the MSV. In his study on the banking business model, which is becoming financialised, he says that the main focus of researchers on financialisation is in the study of the principle of the MSV. Even the banks have surrendered to financialisation, making it clear that such an economic movement was not and is not natural, but a product of decisions and in fact a product, created and sold by consultancy firms and mainstream finance books to be implemented by managers (Erturk, 2015, p.3).

As the search for the valuation of shares is fundamental in this new financialised business model, profitability alone cannot raise the price of shares, hence the need to repurchase options to force an increase in the value of shares and provide 20% return annually. This return is spectacular compared to production profits (in the case of banks the core business of raising and lending money) even when it comes to banks, as demonstrated in the case of Citigroup (Erturk, 2015, p.4). In summary, the author states that this policy of maximising shareholder return is risky, but carried out nonetheless. This behaviour was not affected by the new rules and regulatory initiatives of the banking system, which advocated a less risky and more stable financial market. In reality, the big problem, for Erturk, is the fact that the principle of MSV is more important in organisations, including banking than the search for national or social objectives. According to the author, a property structure should be discussed with remuneration that is socially, economically and democratically adequate to its leaders and the search for a socially more useful banking system (Erturk, 2015, p.12).

The tactic of repurchasing shares to raise their price and then, artificially, receive more dividends for a more valued share, has been happening in several sectors of the world economy, all adept at financialisation. Mazzucato (2014) states that in the biotechnology and pharmaceutical sectors, this share buyback comes in conjunction with a decrease in investments in research and development made by the private sector, which has been using ever-increasing public investments to save on these expenses and thus leaving more to distribute to shareholders, who will practice repurchases or stock buybacks. She quotes Pfizer, that "in 2011, together with the distribution of US\$6.2 billion in dividends, there was a repurchase of more than US\$9 billion in shares, 90% of its net revenue" (Mazzucato, 2014, p.55).

Jürgen Kädtler and Hans Sperling (2002) carried out an important study on the German automotive industry and observed that this process of supremacy and power of the financial markets over German automakers did not happen easily; it was late in relation to the process in the United States and demonstrated great resilience of industrial operations to financial dictates. The authors claim that the MSV policy is seen by official rhetoric as a "review of power relations within firms". And that this struggle would be contrary to the unlimited control that managers had over the company in order to be free from the influence of shareholders, that is, it would be the substitution of managerial domination by the managers' adherence to the interests of shareholders (Kädtler and Sperling, 2002, p.82).

Quoting supporters of the MSV principle, Kädtler and Sperling remind the creators of the concept called Economic Value Added (EVA). Consulting firms such as Stern, Stewart & Company, say, have developed metrics that could reconcile industrial activities and operations with the imperatives of financial practices, even if one had a different pace and dynamics than the other.

> For EVA defenders, such an instrument is
>   The only financial management system that provides employees with a common language across all operations and management functions and allows all managerial decisions to be modelled,

monitored and communicated in a simple and consistent way - always in terms of added value to the shareholder investment. (Stewart, 1999, apud Kädtler and Sperling, 2002, p.82)

The financialisation of the economy, societies and organisations is not a simple or natural process. Scientific effort is needed to understand what it is and how it happens. Many scholars, such as Alfred Rappaport (1981; 2006), for example, see financialisation as a natural process of maximising shareholder value and even propose a general "recipe" for how to achieve goals and be successful. He does not even consider that this economic process can be called financialisation.

Since the 1970s, Rappaport has been a staunch supporter of MSV and has published articles and studies "selecting strategies to create shareholder value" (1981). In 2006, he published the article "Ten ways to create shareholder value" in the *Harvard Business Review* where he discusses what companies must do to be successful. Among the ways to create value are: 1) the policy of not commenting on expectations of earnings; 2) making strategic decisions that maximise the expected value, even with a drop in profitability in the short term; 3) making acquisitions that maximise the expected value, even with a drop in profitability in the short term; 4) managing only assets that maximise value; 5) returning money to shareholders even when there is no feasible possibility of creating value at that moment; 6) rewarding CEOs and other senior executives for being able to deliver superior returns in the long run; 7) rewarding executives at operating units for adding superior value over the years; 8) rewarding middle management and frontline workers for delivering superior performance that is key to creating value; 9) requiring senior executives to be concerned with property risks as much as shareholders and 10) providing investors with information relevant to the creation of value (Rappaport, 2006, pp.3–13).

These principles have been increasingly advocated by investors as being essential to business, remembering that supposedly the risks are exclusive to investors and, therefore, all the reward must fall on them. Note that the reward for workers will be given only to frontline workers and middle management and not to all employees of the company, contrary to the speeches about corporate social responsibility, which highlights the well-being of the entire organisation, or even the principles of total quality, for which everyone has responsibilities for the successes and failures of organisations.

The fact is that the positions are divergent regarding the value judgment of the principle of maximising shareholder value, but most researchers see this process as negative, where there would only be a few rich beneficiaries of such operations to the detriment of a large majority of stakeholders who would have little or nothing to gain.

As William Lazonick (2012) rightly pointed out, from 2001 to 2010, 459 companies listed on the S&P 500 in January 2011 distributed US$1.9 trillion in dividends, or 40% of their net profit and US$2.6 trillion in stock buybacks, 54% of net profit, spent on share buybacks so that they would achieve an artificial appreciation. "After all, what was left over for investments in innovation, including upgrading the capabilities of their workforces? Not much" says Lazonick (2012, p.4).

Financialisation in the automotive sector

The participation of banks and large groups of investors in the controlling interest of automotive companies is a clear indication of the financialisation of the sector. In addition, the automakers themselves have their banks to finance the sale of the automobiles they produce, and these activities are more profitable than the production itself. Examples of these institutions are Fiat Bank, Volkswagen Bank, RCI, (Renault's financial arm), Mercedes-Benz Bank, among others (Anef, 2015). In addition to the banks, there are the financial subsidiaries of the automakers, such as Ford Motor Credit Company LLC, which "offers a wide variety of automotive financial products" in the form of financing or leasing (Ford Motor Company, 2015a, p.8).

The automotive sector represents a powerful slice of the global industry and produces a commodity that has revolutionised human society, the automobile, which has been produced for over a hundred years, arousing passions of all kinds. Furthermore, the gigantic number of figures for the automotive sector draws attention. If it were a country, it would be the sixth-largest GDP in the world (Gabriel et al., 2010, p.2), having moved US$2.5 trillion in 2005. Its influence in other productive chains is such that approximately 50% of the total rubber, 25% of the total glass and 15% of the total steel produced worldwide are destined for this industry (Casotti and Goldenstein, 2008, p.149). In addition to employing around 8 million workers and another 5 million indirect workers to each direct one, employed in the auto parts sector. Worldwide, 10% of developed countries' GDP is attributed to this sector. In Brazil, the auto industry represented in 2011 the impressive share of 18.2% of the Brazilian industrial GDP (Kubota, 2012, p.9), reaching 23% of the industrial GDP in 2013 and 5% of the total GDP (Anfavea, 2015, p.13).

Simultaneously with this success and achievements, a process of transformation is underway that concerns us. The "industry of industries" (Womack et al., 2004) now faces its greatest challenge, which is to continue to be an industrial, productive sector, but with several changes in its structure, not only due to the greater dependence on the financial sector but because of changes caused by globalisation, such as the decrease in the share of production in Europe, the United States and Japan, from 77% of the total in 1997 to 50%, and the increase in production in China from 3% in 1997 to 22% in 2009 (Bailey et al., 2010). Zilbovicius and Marx (2011) highlighted several challenges to the automotive industry at the beginning of the 21st century, in addition to its already traditional problems. Environment, technology, pollution, work organisation, use of land and fossil resources on a large scale are some of the challenges presented to the automotive sector, in addition to economic sustainability. They question what role will be reserved for countries in the new global automotive industry, which is being redesigned and what are the opportunities and threats in the near future for the automobile and its industry (Zilbovicius and Marx, 2011). This is a new concern that, similar to the concerns about the sector's financialisation process, make up another dimension of the same development process for the automotive industry and speculations about its future.

With regard to social and human impacts, studies related to financialisation in the automotive sector have emphasised that this process is too destructive and offensive to the capitalist production method and to society as a whole. This is because the dismissal of workers from the automakers and wage cuts, in addition to the discrepancy between growth in financial assets and growth in hiring and wage increases, may cause an even greater crisis, with the decrease in the consumer market mainly in western Europe and the United States (Elías, 2014, p.2).

According to Elías (2014), financialisation in the automotive sector is defined as an appreciation process that privileges the financial aspects of the operation, making the return to shareholders in the form of dividend payments at the centre of concerns. This Mexican author, Júlio Castellanos Elías, a researcher in the permanent study group on jobs and wages in industry – Gerpisa – based in France, focuses his concerns on the relationship between labour, technological innovation and finance, resuming the debate established by Hyman Minsk in 1985. This debate placed the need for an integrated approach to these three factors of production at the origin of instabilities and stated that the struggle between labour, innovation and finance to capture the bulk of profits has been creating inconsistencies and instabilities that cannot be understood in the typical picture of linear analysis of the three classic production systems supposedly existing: Taylorism, Fordism and Toyotism. For him, following the line of thought of Boyer and Freyssenet (2000), there are at least six types of productive systems, which mixed and complementary work best according to each country, each society and each growth and income system (Elías, 2013b, p.5).

Elías (2013a, p.5) claims that the financialisation variable played a very important role in the collapse of the General Motors Corporation (GMC). According to him, William Lazonick, in his presentation: "The Innovative Enterprise and the Development State: Toward an Economics of 'Organisational Success'", on the occasion of the Annual Bretton Woods Conference, promoted by the Institute for New Economic Thinking, on April 10, 2011, wrote that

> if the three major US automakers had not spent US$50 billion over the last twenty years on impressing Wall Street, they would not have made it to the situation they were in, and if General Motors had stayed in the banks with the US$20.4 billion distributed to stockholders from 1986 to 2002, it would have had US$29.4 billion of its own cash to stay afloat and respond to the global competition when it went broke.
>
> (Elías, 2013b, p.11)

In his other case study on General Motors Elías (2013b), categorically states that the breakdown of GMC was almost programmed, since decisions taken to face cyclical demand difficulties were aimed at privileging financial activities, in addition to cost cuts and layoffs of thousands of workers (Elías, 2013b, p.7). He analyses the numbers of the North American automakers' annual reports and detects several wrong strategic decisions, such as dividends payments of the order of US$22 billion in 15 years, a high and irresponsible value according to him; interest payments in the order of US$139 billion to creditors in 15 years, which corresponds to more than US$9 billion per year, much higher than the annual profit; buying companies that had nothing to do with the core business, only to resell them in the following decade and at a loss; a sale of 51% of GMAC in 2006, which was the financial subsidiary of GM and which yielded more than twice as much as the manufacturing division (Elías, 2013b, p.11).

Still quoting the same author, who has been analysing financialisation in the automotive sector, in his text on Volkswagen Elías (2014) recalls that the increase in financial assets was 413% in 14 years, from 1994 to 2007, while the number of employees grew 172%. This would be another indication of financialisation in the sector.

At Japanese Toyota, the financialisation process has also been studied. Elías and Granados (2015) discuss the development of the automaker and its growth under the aegis of financialisation assumptions. The Japanese company, which initially produced mechanical looms and yarn-making machines, from the mid-19th century until the interwar period, started producing automobiles after the Second World War. It was in the crisis of 1949–1950, with huge indebtedness and worker strikes, that the company was forced to leave its car sales in instalments with the banks and lay off about 30% of the workforce. In addition, the growth of financial assets and liabilities, from 1991 to 2007, according to the authors, is four times greater than the growth of fixed assets, "which shows to a large extent how resources are destined to sustain growth based on finance, that is, financialisation" (Elías and Granados, 2015, p.17).

While in the financial market the rate of return is considerably high, in the automotive sector the rate of return on capital employed and the accumulated value of the investment are considered mediocre compared to the requirements of the stock exchanges (Froud et al., 2002). Table 1.1 shows the accumulated value of GM shares over a five-year period, indicating a poor performance compared to the other indices. As we can see, there was an investment loss of at least 0.54%, without discounting inflation, which, if taken into account, would show an even greater loss to those who invested in the automaker.

This situation demonstrated above causes the financial capital to put pressure on the automotive industry to make greater profits. Such pressures alter the modus operandi of automotive companies, making them prioritise their objectives in financial activities in order to achieve the expected rates of return often 12 to 15%, while in real production the production profits do not exceed 3 to 5% (Froud et al., 2002).

The rates of return on revenues in both the automotive and financial areas are an important component for studying the financialisation of the automotive sector. It is from them that the dimension of the struggle and the pressures that financial capital makes on the automotive industry appears. Financial services represent increasingly important shares of the total activity of the automotive industry.

Table 1.1 Accumulated value of US$100 of capital invested in 2010

US$100	2010	2011	2012	2013	2014	2015
GM	100	54.99	78.21	110.88	98.04	99.46
S&P 500	100	102.11	118.45	156.82	178.28	180.75
Dow Jones 30	100	83.96	104.40	138.58	132.57	131.66

Source: General Motors Annual Report 2015a, p.24.

So much so that financial innovation was developed at Ford, which was the creation of the Ford Motor Credit Company in 1959, and from 1988 onwards data on the financial contribution, as opposed to the contribution from Ford Automotive, began to be released. Froud et al. (2006) demonstrate that the growing role of Ford Financial was not considered in detail by most analysts, but that its development is notorious (Froud et al., 2006, p.265). According to the authors, since 1988 there has been a movement of growth in the participation of the financial area in the contribution index. Ford financial only contributed 12.4% in 1988, with Ford automotive being responsible for 87.6% of the total contribution to the business that year. This would appear to be a predominance of production over finance, but when we note that Ford's financial contribution was 100% in 1991, 1992 and 2001 to 2007, while its productive area had losses of US$50.432 billion just eight years ago, we should consider this process of dependence on the financial sphere that the automotive sector has been presenting (Froud et al., 2006, p.289, tab.c2.5).

The pressure for an increasingly greater return to shareholders and the profitability that the productive activity cannot achieve causes efforts to deviate to any activities that are more profitable, offering other financial "products" to increase their gains. In the case of automakers, the creation of banks and financiers for automobiles to be sold in instalments or leasing is symptomatic of a change in the source of profitability. Only these financial-type activities are able to make profits in significant percentages and thus achieve the investors' objectives.

The criterion for choosing the five largest automakers was given by the production volume indicated by OICA and was adopted due to the size and representativeness that these five automakers have, around 50% of world production. That is, it is a highly oligopolised market, where few companies hold a large share of both production and the consumer market. With just five cases we will be able to get to know most of the current reality of this financialisation process (see Table 1.2).

The five automakers

The **Ford Motor Company** was founded in 1903 by Henry Ford and has been in the automotive market for over a hundred years, currently producing vehicles on six continents. Altogether it has 187 thousand workers spread over 62 plants around the world. Its main brands are Ford and Lincoln and in 2014 the company sold more than 6 million vehicles worldwide, with a total revenue of US$144 billion. The automaker has five continental divisions, established in North America,

Table 1.2 Number of cars produced

Automaker	2014	2015	% 2015
Toyota	10,475,338	10,083,831	11.19
Volkswagen	9,894,891	9,872,424	10.95
General Motors	9,609,326	7,485,587	8.30
Hyundai	8,008,987	7,988,479	8.86
Ford	5,969,541	6,396,369	7.10
Total of the five largest	43,958,083	41,826,690	46.42
World Total	90,717,246	90,086,346	100

Source: World Motor Vehicle Production. International Organization of Motor Vehicle Manufacturers, OICA, 2014, 2015b.

South America, Europe, the Middle East and Africa and Asia and the Pacific, in addition to the financial services division, represented by the Ford Motor Credit Company LLC (Ford Motor Company, 2015a, p.2). In 2014, Ford had a 7.2% share of the global auto market. Its largest individual share was in Canada with 15.5% of the automaker's sales in that country alone. The United States, with 14.7%, England with 14.5%, Argentina with 14.1%, Turkey with 11.7% and Brazil with 9.4% were the countries that most represented the company's sales slices worldwide (Ford Motor Company, 2015a, p.7).

In terms of employment, Ford grew its total hires between 2013 and 2014, from 181 thousand workers in 2013 to 187 thousand in 2014. It grew in North America, from 84 thousand to 90 thousand workers, but decreased in South America, where it dropped from 18,000 to 16,000 employees from one year to the next. The same movement took place in its European division, which reduced its posts from 50 thousand workers to 47 thousand. A strong growth occurred in the Asia and Pacific division, going from 20 thousand workers in 2013 to 25 thousand in 2014, an increase of 25%. Jobs in the Middle East and Africa continued with the same 3,000 workers in the two years in question; the same goes for the Ford Motor Credit Company division, which retained 6,000 employees in both 2013 and 2014 (Ford Motor Company, 2015a, p.13). Although the ratio has grown from one year to the next, historically there has been a huge drop in jobs, as we will see.

For the past 25 years, Ford has been going through an intense financialisation process, expressed by its increasing dependence on financial services as opposed to its production area. **General Motors Corporation** was founded in 1909 in the United States and today it was the third-largest car manufacturer in 2015, worldwide, having reached the mark of 9,958,000 units produced. It has four divisions spread across the planet, which are: GMNA, General Motors North America, responsible for the production of 3,612,000 units in 2015; GME, General Motors Europe, responsible for 1,176,000 units manufactured; GMIO, General Motors International Operations (Asia/Pacific/Middle East/Africa), which produced 4,525,000 units and lastly GMSA, General Motors South America, whose production was 645,000 units (General Motors Corporation, 2015a, p.2).

GM's share of the world auto market is stable but pointing to a slight drop over the past three years, having accounted for 11.5% in 2013, 11.4% in 2014 and 11.2% of the world market in 2015. This drop occurred in all divisions, except for the international division, which includes Asia/Pacific, Middle East and Africa, which had a slight increase, going from 9.8% of participation in these markets in 2013 to 10.3% in 2015. The Chinese market has been growing in the share of GM, representing 14.9% of all its sales in 2015, only behind the United States (17.3%) and Brazil, responsible for 15.1% of participation in the automaker's global market (General Motors Corporation, 2015a, p.2).

In terms of employment, GM has been decreasing its job levels for many years. We will see later that from the end of the 1980s onwards the North American automaker cut two-thirds of its workforce, which was 766 thousand workers in 1988 and reached 215 thousand in 2015. In the last three years, it went from 219 thousand in 2013 to 216 thousand in 2014 and 215 thousand in 2015. Only the North American division saw growth, from 109 thousand workers in 2013 to 110 thousand in 2014 and 115 thousand in 2015. In addition to this division, GM Finance also grew its jobs, from 6 thousand workers in 2013 to 7 thousand in 2014 and 8 thousand employees in 2015 (General Motors Corporation, 2015, p.10).

The European division reduced its jobs from 37 thousand in 2013 to 36 thousand in 2015. The division of Asia, the Middle East and Africa also, from 36 thousand workers in 2013 to 32 thousand in 2015 and the most suffered cuts was the southern division -American, which dropped from 31 thousand jobs in 2013 to 24 thousand in 2015, 23% less (General Motors Corporation, 2015a, p.10).

The company was bailed out by the US government in 2009 to avoid bankruptcy and mass layoffs. The government held 31% of the shareholding, which was later sold in 2013 when the automaker was able to recover, keep most jobs and make a profit again.

The automaker **Hyundai Motor Company** is part of the conglomerate Hyundai Motor Group, which is a giant of the South Korean industry, with 2015 revenue of US$217.275 billion. With a net profit of US$12.949 billion, the Hyundai Group employed 262,463 people in 2015. This group operates in several sectors of the economy, with the auto industry alone accounting for 53% of its revenues, 61% of net income and 64% of their workforce (Hyundai, 2016a).

The auto parts sector represents the second activity, with 21% of revenues and 25% of net income, followed by civil construction, with 8% of revenues and the steel sector, which accounts for 7% of its revenues. Finances represent 3% of revenues, 3% of net profits and 4% of labour (Hyundai, 2016a).

Started in 1947 as a construction company, Hyundai (modern in Korean) is called *chaebol*, a family conglomerate led by a parent company. From the construction sector, it underwent a diversification process, reaching the automotive sector in 1967, with the creation of Hyundai Motors. In 1973, it entered the heavy industry business. In 1976, it founded Hyundai Merchant Marine and Hyundai General Trade. The financial business came with Hyundai Insurance in 1977. The diversification strategy did not stop and together with government partnerships, the group grew visibly.

Youngjae Lim (2002) highlighted three moments in the history of the Hyundai group, since its expansion, from 1947 to 1979, going through the period from 1980 to 1998 (with the establishment of Hyundai Electronics, in 1983; Hyundai Elevators, in 1984; Hyundai Oil Refining, in 1993 and Hyundai Investments in 1998) until its division in several subgroups, from 2001. This made the Hyundai group become the largest industrial group in South Korea (Lim, 2002, p.5). All, of course, with substantial state incentives, coupled with a favourable change in the international market that has made South Korean products and services increasingly present abroad (Green, 1992).

After the developmental period, the Asian crisis of 1997–1998 and the death of the founder of the group Chung Ju Yung, an internal struggle started for the control of the gigantic company. Four children and two nephews vied for power in the main companies, which became subgroups, to see who would stay with the most profitable business, emphasising the so-called core business, with some subsidiaries being handed over to creditor banks, such as the founder Hyundai Constructions, Hyundai Electronics and Hyundai Investments (Lim, 2002).

From the end of the 90s until now, the company acquired Kia Motors in 1998 and in the 2000s it developed the Hyundai Card-Life-Capital-Commercial division, which although was responsible for only 3% of the net profit in 2015, has superior profitability compared to the productive segment, except for Hyundai Life, which has been making losses since 2012.

Toyota Motor Corporation is a limited liability company incorporated under the Japan Commercial Code and continues to exist under the terms of the Commercial Companies Act. It started operations in 1933 as the automobile division of Toyota Industries Corporation (formerly Toyoda Automatic Loom Works, Ltd.). It became a separate company on 28 August 1937. In 1982, the Toyota Motor Company and Toyota Motor Sales were merged into a single company, which is Toyota Motor Corporation today. As of 31 March 2015, Toyota operated through 541 consolidated subsidiaries (including entities of variable interest) and 203 associated companies, of which 54 companies were accounted for using the equity method (Toyota Motors Corporation, 2015, p.8).

Its products are sold in more than 190 countries and its main markets in 2015 were North America (30.3%), Japan (24% of sales), Asia (16.6%), Europe (9.6%) and the remaining 19.5% are distributed between the regions of South and Central America, Africa, Oceania and the Middle East (Toyota Motors Corporation, 2015, p.9).

The automaker produced 10,083,831 vehicles in 2015, a drop from the previous year, which reached 10,475,338 units, making it the largest automaker on the planet. Its revenue in Japanese currency (yen) increased from 25.691 trillion to 27.234 trillion yen, but the large devaluation of the yen against the dollar from 2014 to 2015 (when it went from JPY 102.00 per dollar to JPY 120.17 per dollar in March 2015) dropped Toyota's revenue from US$249 billion in 2014 to US$226 billion in 2015. Otherwise, its revenue would reach US$267 billion in 2015, were the yen at the JPY 102 level per US$1 verified in 2014.

The giant Japanese automaker has been developing a quick process of financialising its activities, expressed by its growing dependence on financial institutions and investors, which increasingly demand a return on their investments. Dividends payments to shareholders are the main indicators of financialisation and have demonstrated Toyota's commitment to the assumptions of financial logic.

The automaker **Volkswagen** (people's car) was founded in 1937 by the German state and was the second largest car producer in the world in 2014. Moreover, 9,894,891 units were produced, with a workforce of 592,586 employees. There was an increase of 5% in production and 3.5% in employment compared to the previous year, 2013. In 2015, there was a decrease of more than 20 thousand units, with production falling 1.9% compared to 2014. The company produced 9,872,424 automobiles in 2015 with a volume of 610,076 workers, a 3% increase in employment compared to the previous year.

Its biggest markets were Europe, where it sold 4,392,000 cars, with a 4.5% growth; Asia-Pacific, with sales of 4,058,000 vehicles, an increase of 11.3% in this region compared to 2013. In China alone, 3,668,433 units were sold, that is, 90% of all consumption of the automaker's

Asia-Pacific region (Volkswagen, 2015a, p.97). In North America, there was a small increase in sales, of 0.2%, with 893 thousand cars sold. The automaker's major loss was in South America, with a 19.9% drop in sales, which dropped to 795 thousand units in 2014 compared to a sale of 992 thousand units in 2013 (Volkswagen, 2014, p.21). VW has 100 factories around the world, distributed in 27 countries.

The Volkswagen Aktiengesellschaft Group (listed in stock exchange) consists of two divisions: the automotive division and the financial services division. The automotive division is made up of 12 brands, which are: VW passenger vehicles; VW commercial vehicles; SEAT; SKODA, Audi; Bentley; Porsche; Scania; MAN, Ducati, Bugatti and Lamborghini.

The Financial Division, "which corresponds to the financial services segment combines commerce and customer services, financing activities, leasing, banking and insurance services, fleet management and mobility offers" (Volkswagen, 2014, p.21).

In 2015, the company suffered a huge setback, with the public disclosure of a fraud scandal in the results of CO_2 emission tests on its vehicles, known as the diesel gate scandal, involving 11 million cars produced between 2009 and 2015. It is estimated that VW is expected to spend around 6.5 billion euros on recalls and repairs on adulterated cars. The scandal led to the dismissal of CEO Martin Winterkorn, accused of knowing everything and hiding the truth. It also led to a drop in the share price from €253.20 on 10 April 2015, to €92.36 on 2 October of the same year (Investing, 2016).

2 Profits obtained through financial activities versus profits obtained through productive activities

Now we will compare the sources of profitability in the automakers through the contrast between profits obtained through financial activities and profits obtained through productive activities. We use data from the annual reports for 2001 to 2018. In some automakers, we did not have all these years available, but we managed to get most of them.

Ford

It should be mentioned that 2014 was one of the largest proportional differences in the Ford sector revenue. Total revenues reached US$144.077 billion, with revenues from the company's manufacturing sector totalling US$135.782 billion, with a profit of US$2.548 billion, or just a 1.9% return on revenue. In the financial sector, there was a revenue of US$8.295 billion with a profit of US$1.794 billion, a 21% return on revenues. In 2010, this had already happened, with a return of the productive area of 3.4% and a return of the financial area that reached 34%, as we will see later.

When we look back and forth at Ford's revenues, we see that, like other automakers, this is a cyclical movement and very susceptible to fluctuations in demand, and in recent years it has left total revenues of US$160 billion in 2001 to US$177 billion in 2005, falling to US$118 billion in 2009, just after the North American subprime crisis. Ford only recovered its US$160 billion levels in 2018. The most interesting thing to note is that when we look at the net profit value of any year, we cannot immediately see what the composition of that profit is. In a closer analysis of the company's annual report, we see that in 2010 the gross profit of US$7.069 billion comprised US$4.066 billion from Ford Automotive and US$3.003 billion from Ford Financial (Ford Motor Company, 2015a).

DOI: 10.4324/9781003161141-2

That is, almost 45% of the profit came from financial activities and around 55% of the profit was obtained through productive activities. This may seem like a predominance of profitability from the production area, with more than half of the total profitability, but when we analyse the proportion of profit in relation to the revenues of each sector, we see that Ford Financial wins and, by far it has been winning, in terms of profitability, compared to Ford Automotive, as we can see in Table 2.1.

It is in demonstrating this difference in the percentage of return that we intend to focus on now. The automaker's financial services were, on average, ten times more profitable than its production area, factories and other facilities. Although from 2015 to 2018 the returns in relation to the revenues of the productive sector reached higher percentages, such as 5.8% in 2015 and 6.6% in 2016, they remained at low levels, declining to 4.9% in 2017 and 3.6% in 2018. Meanwhile, returns on the automaker's financial sector revenues were 22% in 2015, 18% in 2016, 20% in 2017 and 22% in 2018. This is an unmistakable manifestation

Table 2.1 Ford revenues by sector

	Total revenue in billions of US$	Automotive sector revenues	Profit before tax	% return/ revenue	Financial sector revenues	Profit before tax	% return/ revenue
2001	**160,504**	130,736	**−8.857**	**−6.7**	29,768	1,438	**4.8**
2002	**162,256**	134,273	**−1,153**	**−0.8**	27,983	2.104	**7.5**
2003	**164,196**	138,442	**−1,957**	**−1.1**	25,754	3,327	**13**
2004	**171,646**	147,128	**−0,155**	**−0.1**	24,518	5.008	**20**
2005	**177,089**	153,503	**−3,895**	**−2.5**	23,586	5,891	**25**
2006	**160,123**	143,307	**−17.017**	**−11.8**	16,816	1,966	**12**
2007	**170,572**	154,379	**−5.081**	**−3.2**	16,193	1,224	**7.5**
2008	**145,114**	129,165	**−11,917**	**−9.2**	15.949	**−2.581**	**−16**
2009	**118,308**	105,893	1,212	**1.1**	12,415	1.814	**14**
2010	**128,122**	119.28 0	4,066	**3.4**	8,842	3.003	**34**
2011	**135,605**	128,168	6.215	**4.9**	7.437	2,431	**33**
2012	**133,559**	126,567	5.928	**4.7**	6,992	1,710	**25**
2013	**146,917**	139,369	5.368	**3.8**	7.548	1,672	**22**
2014	**144,077**	135,782	2,548	**1.9**	8.295	1,794	**21**
2015	**149,558**	140,566	8.224	**5.8**	8,992	2,028	**22**
2016	**151,800**	141,546	9,422	**6.6**	10,253	1.820	**18**
2017	**156,776**	145,653	7.259	**4.9**	11,113	2,248	**20**
2018	**160,338**	148,294	5.422	**3.6**	12,018	2,627	**22**

Source: Ford Annual Reports: (Ford Motor Company, 2003, pp.66–67, 2005, p.54, 2006, p.49, 2009, pp.74–75, 2012, p.63, 2014, p.27, 2015a, p.26, 2016, p.84, 2017, p.81, 2018, pp. 26, 77).

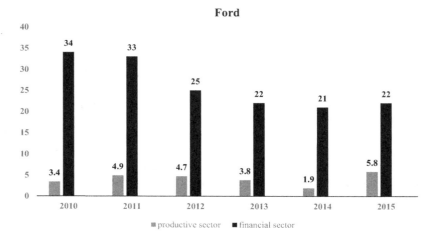

Figure 2.1 Comparison between the sources of profitability in % – Ford
Source: authors, based on the automakers' annual reports.

of the financialisation process in contemporary companies, and the automotive industry is becoming involved in this process in a very visible way. If we compare 2001 when the financial sector had revenues of US$29 billion and profit before taxes of US$1.4 billion, the result was a 4.8% return. In 2018, with a lower revenue of US$12 billion, there was a pre-tax profit of US$2.6 billion, or 22% return on revenue. That is, even in the financial sector of the automaker, there has been an increase in profitability in proportion to the revenue.

Figure 2.1 clearly shows this distinction between Ford automaker's sources of profitability. If we take 2010, the brutal difference also occurs. Productive sector revenues were US$119.280 billion and a profit of US$4.066 billion, resulting in a 3.4% rate of return. Meanwhile, the company's financial sector revenues that same year were US$8.842 billion and its profit of US$3.003 billion, that is, 34% of return!

From 1988 to 2003, a period comprising sixteen years, Ford Financial's contribution was greater than that of Ford Automotive in ten years, having collaborated over five years with 100% of the company's profit, since Ford automotive made losses of US$5.477 billion in 1991, US$2.562 billion in 1992, US$9.394 billion in 2001, US$1.181 billion in 2002 and US$1.957 billion in 2003 (Froud et al., 2006, p.289, Table C2.5,). Table 2.2 shows these numbers.

Table 2.2 Ford's contribution by sector

	Contribution of automotive sector		Contribution of financial sector	
	US$ billions	*%*	*US$ billions*	*%*
1988	11,378	87.6	1,604	12.4
1989	7,655	85.5	1,298	14.5
1990	0,387	18.4	1,719	81.6
1991	**−5,477**	**0**	**1,980**	**100**
1992	**−2,562**	**0**	**2,395**	**100**
1993	1,645	32.3	3,456	67.7
1994	7,449	68.2	3,468	31.8
1995	3,825	47.2	4,276	52.8
1996	3,019	37.8	4,957	62.2
1997	8,129	64.7	4,427	35.3
1998	7,860	27.4	20,829	72.6
1999	9,337	76.6	2,851	23.4
2000	5,631	64	3,172	36.0
2001	**−9,394**	**0**	**1,509**	**100**
2002	**−1,181**	**0**	**2,155**	**100**
2003	**−1,957**	**0**	**3,327**	**100**
2004	**−0,200**	**0**	**5,000**	**100**
2005	**−3,900**	**0**	**5,000**	**100**
2006	**−17,000**	**0**	**2,000**	**100**
2007	**−5,000**	**0**	**1,200**	**100**
2008	**−11,800**	**0**	**−2,600**	**0**
2009	0,785	30	1,814	70
2010	4,146	55	3,003	45
2011	6,215	71.5	2,431	28.5
2012	5,928	77	1,710	23
2013	5,368	77	1,672	23
2014	2,548	59	1,794	41
2015	8,224	80	2,028	20

Sources: Froud et al. (2006) and Ford Annual Reports, several years.

Note: Ford's automotive sector had losses of US$50.43 billion in just eight years, from 2001 to 2008.

In the 2000s, the results were also not positive until 2009, when the company stopped the process of annual losses and resumed profitability. Moreover, in those years, the financial sector saved the company. In 2004, against a US$200 million loss from Ford Automotive, Ford Financial earned US$5 billion in revenue. In 2005, Ford Automotive's further losses of US$3.9 billion were only offset by Ford Financial's US$5 billion profit. In 2006, the Ford Automotive's US$17 billion loss could not be saved by Ford Financial's US$2 billion profit. In 2007, there was a loss of US$5 billion from Ford Automotive and a small profit from Ford Financial of US$1.2 billion. Only in 2008, during a crisis in the North American real estate market, did both Ford Automotive and Ford Financial show losses of US$11.8 billion and US$2.6 billion, respectively.

In 25 years, at least 12 years showed losses on the part of Ford Automotive with exclusive contribution from Ford Financial and in the remaining 13 years, when there was profit, Ford Financial profitability was approximately ten times greater than that of Ford Automotive.

Besides, when we look at the accumulated value over five years, Ford made a loss for those who invested US$100 in their stocks in 2010, generating US$94 in 2015. Devaluation of 6% in five years, without discounting the average inflation of the 2010–2015 period, which was around 1.7% per year (US Inflation Calculator, 2016). Meanwhile, the S&P 500 and Dow Jones Automobiles & Parts Titans 30 indexes achieved an incredible 81% and 32% appreciation, respectively, an average of 16% per year for S&P and 6% for the Dow Jones 30 (see Table 2.3).

These figures illustrate the fact that there is a conscious option for the intensification of the company's financial services, through its subsidiary Ford Motor Credit Company LLC, involving instalment sales in the medium and even long term, leasing and other purchase options, which are of vital importance in the profitability of the company and even means a real lifeline in the periods of crisis and huge losses already seen in the company's history. These financed, instalment or leased sales represented 38% of the total in 2012 and increased to 45% in 2014, only in the United States. Other interesting data that illustrate the financialisation process is that of the company's assets. In 2014, total assets were US$210.443 billion, of which US$121 billion were financial assets and only US$90 billion were fixed assets in the automotive sector. More than 60% of the assets originated from Ford Financial.

This leads us to ask: what economic strategy has Ford been adopting? When the company's profits come from financial activities, from credit,

Table 2.3 Accumulated value of US$100 of capital invested in 2010 – Ford

US$100	2010	2011	2012	2013	2014	2015
Ford	100	64	79	96	100	94
S&P 500	100	102	118	157	178	181
Dow Jones 30	100	84	104	139	133	132

Source: Ford Motor Company, Annual Report, 2015a, p.200.

interest and typical activities of banks and other financial organisations, we can reflect: what is happening with this industrial segment today? These concerns will be raised when we discuss the analysis of maximising shareholder value. The pressure from shareholders and senior executives and directors of the company for an even greater return is combined with the conscious option of capital appreciation through financial activities, which can have serious consequences for real production, employment, wages, workers and other stakeholders.

General Motors

General Motors' revenue mix is close to Ford's revenue history, with the difference that GM had sold 51% of its financial division, GMAC, in 2006, and after the US government bailout in 2009, restructured its production bases and its relationship with the financial area. Even so, the profitability of its financial sector has always been proportionally greater than that of its productive sector. Since 2010, its share of financial services in total revenues has grown nominally, although it has fallen as an index related to profitability compared to revenues. In 2010, revenues from the productive sector were US$135.3 billion, with a profit of US$6.9 billion, that is, 5.1% of return on revenue in the production area. In the same year, the financial sector's revenues were the meagre US$281 million, but they showed a profit of US$129 million, or 45.9% of return on revenue, exactly nine times greater than the return of the productive area. See these data in Table 2.4.

Table 2.4 General Motors revenue by sector

	2010	2011	2012	2013	2014	2015
Total Revenue in billions of US$	135,592	150,276	152,256	155,427	155,929	152,356
Revenues of automotive sector in billions of US$	135,311	148,866	150,295	152,092	151,092	145,922
profit before tax	6,901	7,682	7,116	7,680	5,696	9,987
% return on revenue	**5.1**	**5.1**	**4.7**	**5.0**	**3.7**	**6.8**
Revenues of financial sector in billions of US$	0,281	1,410	1,961	3,335	4,837	6,434
profit before tax	0,129	0,622	0,744	0,898	0,803	0,837
% return on revenue	**45.9**	**44.1**	**37.9**	**26.9**	**16.6**	**13.0**

Source: General Motors Annual Reports: Select Financial Data, 2011, pp.195, 196; 2014, pp.28, 35, 131; 2015a, pp.23, 29, 102.

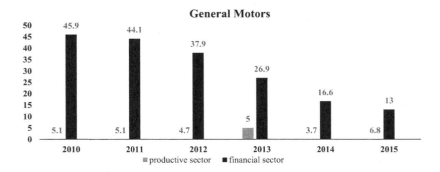

Figure 2.2 Comparison between the sources of profitability in % – GM
Source: authors, based on the automakers' annual reports.

Financial income multiplied by five, from US$281 million in 2010 to US$1.410 billion in 2011, with profits of US$622 million, a 44% return on the financial sector revenue. Moreover, they have not stopped growing, rising to US$1.961 billion in 2012, US$3.335 billion in 2013, US$4.837 billion in 2014 and US$6.434 billion in 2015, with a profit of US$837 million, or 13% return on revenue from the financial sector, much lower than that at the beginning of the 2010s, when it exceeded 45% this year, but even so twice the return on revenue from the productive sector, which was 6.8% in 2015 as we can see in Figure 2.2.

Table 2.5 shows the participation of each sector in the contribution to the business from 2004 to 2015. Until 2006, the financial sector was responsible for a significant share of revenues. It should be noted that the data show, from 2004 to 2009, figures referring to the gross revenue of each sector, since we did not find the data on earnings before taxes, the EBIT. It was only after 2009 that the company started to detail its financial sector. From 2010 to 2015, the data refer to the EBIT for each sector.

In terms of the accumulated value of capital, for every US$100, when we speak not of the profitability of each sector, but return on the capital invested, GM has been bringing losses to the investor. Table 2.6 shows the evolution of investment from 2010 to 2015. Moreover, it compares US$100 at GM stock with the other index in stock exchanges.

These figures demonstrate that studies claiming that automakers' profitability is mediocre compared to stock market indexes are true and are supported by observable reality. Those who invested US$100 in GM in 2010 had a nominal loss of 0.54% in five years, without discounting

Table 2.5 General Motors' contribution by sector

	Contribution of GM Automotive in billions of US$	%	Contribution of Financial GM in billions of US$	%
2004	163,341*	83.62	32,010*	16.38
2005	160,228*	82.32	34,427*	17.68
2006	170,651*	83.47	33,816*	16.53
2007	177,594*	98.68	2,390*	1.32
2008	147,732*	99.17	1,247*	0.83
2009	104,106*	100	—	0
2010	6,901**	98.17	0,129**	1.83
2011	7,682**	92.51	0,622**	7.49
2012	7,116**	90.54	0,744**	9.46
2013	7,680**	89.54	0,898**	10.46
2014	5,696**	87.65	0,803**	12.35
2015	9,987**	91.62	0,837**	8.38

Source: General Motors Annual Reports. Multiple years.

* Gross revenue from both sectors; in November 2006, GM sold 51% of GMAC, its financial division; in July 2009, 31% of its shares were purchased by the US government. ** EBIT for both sectors.

Table 2.6 Accumulated value of US$100 of capital invested in 2010 – GM

US$100	2010	2011	2012	2013	2014	2015
GM	100	54.99	78.21	110.88	98.04	99.46
S&P 500	100	102.11	118.45	156.82	178.28	180.75
Dow Jones 30	100	83.96	104.40	138.58	132.57	131.66

Source: General Motors Annual Report, 2015a, p.24.

inflation, which in the United States has been low, at around 1.7% per year in the period 2010/2015 (US Inflation Calculator, 2016). The stock exchanges showed a return of 80.5% in the case of the S&P 500 index and 31.6% in the Dow Jones 30 index, for those who invested the same US$100 in 2010.

Hyundai Motors

Hyundai Motors' revenues come from its productive sector and its financial divisions, comprising Capital, Card, Life and Commercial. We will see that in the case of Hyundai the composition of revenues in the total business is slightly different from the automakers previously analysed, i.e., Ford and GM. While in North America, the productive sector is very unprofitable, in Hyundai it is much more profitable. From 2010 to 2015, Hyundai's production sector showed a return on revenue of 11.71% on average per year. It is much higher than the North American ones, which were around 4% to 5% per year. This may be because, as Hyundai is a manufacturing conglomerate, it is the only automaker in the world that is part of a group that owns a steel company, Hyundai Steel, and which is important for production cost savings, as it has cheaper access to inputs such as sheet metal and other materials for the manufacturing of automobiles. Compared to its financial sector, the commercial division is the one that has performed best, with an average return on revenue of 22% per year.

Table 2.7 shows these complete data from 2010 to 2015.

Table 2.7 Hyundai revenues by sector

	2010	2011	2012	2013	2014	2015
Automotive sector revenues						
Billions of US$	98,858*	67,827	73,644	76,118	77,783	80,173
Profit before tax	9,177	10,117	9,108	10,197	8,675	7,374
% return on revenue	**9.28**	**14.91**	**12.36**	**13.39**	**11.15**	**9.19**
Financial sector revenues						
Hyundai Capital						
Billions of US$	2,665	3,028	3,106	2,804	2,625	2,575
Profit before tax	0,603	0,603	0,512	0,457	0,288	0,325
% return on revenue	**22.62**	**19.91**	**16.48**	**16.29**	**10.86**	**12.62**
Hyundai Card revenues						
Billions of US$	2,021	2,110	2,213	2,215	2,294	2,325
Profit before tax	0,345	0,283	0,203	0,191	0,263	0,210
% return on revenue	**17.07**	**13.41**	**9.17**	**8.62**	**11.46**	**9.03**
Hyundai Life revenues						
Billions of US$	0,898	1,008	0,876	0,636	0,930	1,338
Profit before tax	0,004	0,004	−0,035	−0,035	−0,066	−0,042
% return on revenue	**0.44**	**0.39**	**−3.99**	**−5**	**−7**	**−3**
Hyundai Commercial revenues						
Billions of US$	0,209	0,283	0,303	0,303	0,307	0,323
Profit before tax	0,074	0,087	0,058	0,052	0,036	0,062
% return on revenue	**35.40**	**30.74**	**19.14**	**17.16**	**11.72**	**19.19**

Source: Hyundai Annual Report 2014, pp.3–7; 2012, p.72 and Hyundai Card-Life-Capital-Commercial Annual Report 2014, pp.12–16; Annual Report 2016a, pp.22–35. Percentage calculations were developed by the authors.

* Kia included.

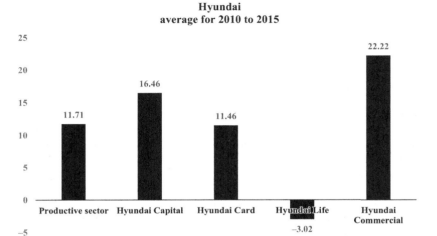

Figure 2.3 Comparison between the sources of profitability in % – Hyundai
Source: authors, based on the automaker's annual reports.

As Table 2.7 demonstrates, the numbers of the financial divisions are better than the numbers of the productive area. The clear exception is Hyundai Life, which has had deficits since 2012, accumulating annual losses of more than 3% of revenue. Hyundai Card presented an annual profit before taxes around a substantial 11.46% of revenue, close to 11.7% of the automaker's production area.

It should be remembered that the productive sector of the Hyundai Motor Company is, until now in our study, the one that has more profitability among the automakers (annual average of 11.7% in six years), when compared to Ford (annual average of 4% in six years – 2010/2015) and GM (average of 5% during the same time). We will see GM's position compared to Toyota and Volkswagen later. See Hyundai's data in Figure 2.3.

When compared to Hyundai Commercial, it has a huge advantage over the production area. The commercial division has been averaging 22% profit before tax annually. This division is responsible for financing commercial vehicles and construction machinery. Loans and leasing are a large part of the business. Meanwhile, in the productive area, profits have been falling year after year. In 2011, there was a 14.91% profit before tax in relation to revenue. Four years later, in 2015, that profit dropped to 9.19%, that is, a 39% drop.

Table 2.8 Hyundai's contribution by sector

	Contribution of Hyundai Automotive in billions of US$	%	Contribution of Hyundai Financial in billions of US$	%
2004	2,605	**81.23**	0,602	**18.77**
2005	3,163	**86.71**	0,485	**13.29**
2006	1,410	**64.48**	0,777	**35.52**
2007	2,074	**76.96**	0,621	**23.04**
2008	1,190	**65.53**	0,626	**34.47**
2009	4,759	**86.34**	0,753	**13.66**
2010	9,177	**89.95**	1,026	**10.05**
2011	10,117	**91.2**	0,977	**8.8**
2012	9,108	**92.51**	0,738	**7.49**
2013	10,197	**93.88**	0,665	**6.12**
2014	8,675	**94.34**	0,521	**5.66**
2015	7,374	**93.01**	0,555	**6.99**

Source: Hyundai Annual Reports, several years.

Table 2.8 shows the contribution of each sector of Hyundai to the business from 2004 to 2015. The financial sector comprises the Card, Capital, Life and Commercial divisions, which together added up to the values described below.

May we remind the reader that we are comparing two sectors of the same family-based conglomerate, which has a broader area of activity than the automotive sector, which represents around 60% of the entire business. Hyundai's financial area is small compared to the entire conglomerate, around 3% to 4%, but when we isolate only the automotive and financial sectors, things change. We can see that from 2006 to 2008, the participation of the financial sector in comparison to the productive sector was 23% to 35% contribution, rates that are not small. In the 2010s, however, there is a continuous decrease of the financial sector in the contribution of these two sectors to the general business, around 5% to 10% of the contribution. In addition, it seems that the financial sector has been in a volume of US$500 million to US$1 billion in contribution to the business for 12 years, i.e., stabilised, while the productive sector of the automaker had much greater variations in that same period, going from US$1.4 billion in 2006 to US$10.197 in 2013, a jump of almost seven times. The fact is that although we consider Hyundai's financialisation late in relation to other automakers, the contribution of the financial sector to the business cannot be ignored, and it has been playing an important role in the years when the automaker's productive area showed more mediocre profits, as it did from 2006 to 2008.

However, we can see from the data presented that Hyundai's productive sector is much more profitable and prevalent in the business as a whole than in competing North American automakers, as was evident in the cases of Ford and General Motors, much more dependent on the financial sector than the South Korean Hyundai. This seems to be a different characteristic of a newer automaker, with the family origin and developed in a country that has relations between the state and private initiatives which are very different from the United States of America. This indicator showed different dynamics that financialisation imposes on different companies within different countries and social structures.

Toyota

Toyota's revenue has been increasing year after year. Despite changes in the exchange rate, such as those which occurred from 2014 to 2015, the picture in recent years is one of revenue growth. Much is due to the growth of the market in North America and Asia, mainly in China.

When we look at Toyota's revenues, we see a situation similar to that of North American automakers and different from that of Hyundai, for example. At Toyota, financial activities yield far greater profits than productive activities, as at Ford and GM.

Table 2.9 shows the total revenues, revenues from the automotive sector, as well as revenues from the automaker's financial sector.

Table 2.9 Toyota revenues by sector

	2010	2011	2012	2013	2014	2015
Total revenue in billions of US$	**215,916**	**238,314**	**237,421**	**234,289**	**249,472**	**226,633**
Automotive sector revenues						
in billions of US$	195,937	217,532	212,910	209,169	224,628	208,555
profit before tax	−0,984	1,078	0,271	9,677	18,312	19,350
% return on revenue	**−0.5**	**0.49**	**0.12**	**4.62**	**8.15**	**9.27**
Financial sector revenues						
in billions of US$	14,189	14,958	13,785	11,992	13,422	13,823
profit before tax	2,813	4,495	3,839	3,235	2,785	3,011
% return on revenue	**19.82**	**30.05**	**27.84**	**26.97**	**20.74**	**21.77**

Source: Toyota Annual Report, 2014, p. 44–47.

Exchange rate available at: www.x-rates.com/calculator/?from=USD&to=JPY& amount=1. $1 = JPY 105.87 in 2014; JPY 97.62 in 2013; JPY 79.82 in 2012; JPY 79.70 in 2011; JPY 87.77 in 2010.

Let's take 2011 as symptomatic and extreme. In this year, the automotive sector made a pre-tax profit of just over US$1 billion, resulting in a meagre 0.49% return on revenue. The financial sector, meanwhile, had a US$4.4 billion pre-tax profit, with a 30% return on revenue. In 2010, Toyota's productive sector had already lost US$984 million, and the financial sector had a profit of US$2.8 billion, that is, 19.82% of return on revenue. This fact has to do with the 2008/2009 crisis, which brought down markets around the world, including the car market.

After that, Toyota embarked on a resumption of profitability in the productive sector, with a profit before tax of US$9.6 billion in 2013, representing a 4.62% return on revenue. Even so, the financial sector posted a profit of US$3.2 billion, an incredible 26.97% return on financial sector revenues.

In 2014, the company grew its profit before taxes in the production area, even more, earning US$18.3 billion, which represented 8.15% of return on revenue. In the financial sector, there were profits before tax of US$2.7 billion, which, on revenue of US$13.4 billion, meant a 20.74% return on revenue (see Figure 2.4).

In recent years, the contribution of the financial sector to the company's business has grown. Although erratically, without indicating a safe trend, in some moments representing more and in others less, the financial contribution remains constant, serving as indispensable help in times when the productive area gives losses or mediocre profits. In

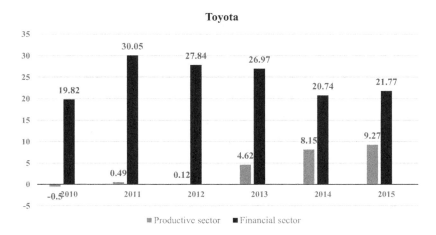

Figure 2.4 Comparison between the sources of profitability in % – Toyota
Source: authors, based on the automakers' annual reports.

Table 2.10 Toyota's contribution by sector

	Contribution of Toyota Automotive in billions of US$	%	Contribution of Toyota Financial in billions of US$	%
2004	13,808	**91.24**	1,327	**8.76**
2005	13,204	**87.86**	1,825	**12.14**
2006	14,603	**91.58**	1,343	**8.42**
2007	17,133	**92.80**	1,331	**7.20**
2008	21,086	**96.18**	0,839	**3.82**
2009	−4,245	**84.60**	−0,773	**15.40**
2010	−0,984	**0**	2,813	**100**
2011	1,078	**20.00**	4,495	**80.00**
2012	0,271	**6.60**	3,839	**93.40**
2013	9,677	**75.00**	3,235	**25.00**
2014	18,312	**86.80**	2,785	**13.20**
2015	19,350	**86.55**	3,011	**13.45**

Source: Toyota Annual Reports, several years.

In 2006, US$1 = JPY 116; in 2007 US$1 = JPY 119; in 2008 US$1 = JPY 103 and in 2009 US$1 = JPY 93. In 2015 US$1 = JPY 120.17. Available at: www.x-rates.com/average/?fro m=USD&to=JPY&amount=1&year=2009

this respect, Toyota has similarities with Ford and GM, although it has suffered losses much less often than its North American competitors (two years in twelve years only). Table 2.10 shows the contribution that each sector made to Toyota's business over 12 years.

From 2004 until 2015, Toyota had only two years of loss in its productive sector, 2009 and 2010, very different from Ford and GM, which already suffered several years of loss in the productive sector. This is directly linked to the global economic crisis triggered by the North American housing market and had affected the Japanese company. In 2009, a critical year, the automaker's financial sector also made a loss, which reached US$773 million, but much smaller than the loss of the automotive sector, which was US$4.2 billion. Overall, the financial sector had a small share in the company's loss. In 2010, with the continued loss in the automotive sector, of US$984 million, the financial sector made profits of US$2.8 billion, bearing 100% of the participation. This picture was repeated until 2012. In 2011, the automotive sector made profits before tax of US$1.078 billion, while the financial sector made profits of US$4.4 billion, accounting for 80% of that year's profit. The same thing happened in 2012, when the automotive sector made profits of only US$271 million and its financial sector profited US$3.8 billion, being responsible for 93.4% of contribution to the business.

From 2013 onwards the numbers seem to have stabilised at the 85/15% ratio between the automotive and financial sectors, similar to the levels found in 2005.

Volkswagen

Volkswagen's total revenues have been growing year after year, similarly to the other four automakers studied here. They went from €126.8 billion in 2010 to €213.2 billion in 2015. An increase of around 60% in just five years.

However, unlike the automakers Ford, GM and Toyota, Volkswagen presents a small difference between the profits from the financial activities in comparison with the profits from the productive activities. Although the differences between these two sources of profitability are small, financial activities have profitability slightly higher than the profit from productive activities, as we can see in Table 2.11.

While in the productive area of Volkswagen the profit before taxes, in the six years between 2010 and 2015, was on average 4.5%, in the financial area the profits before tax were on average 7.5%, almost 70% higher than the performance of the productive sector, but well below Ford, GM and Toyota, which showed differences in profitability that reached a four to ten times advantage for the financial sector. Moreover, it falls short of Hyundai, which had an advantage in the financial area over the productive area. See Volkswagen's sources of profitability in Figure 2.5.

Table 2.11 Volkswagen revenues by sector

	2010	2011	2012	2013	2014	2015
Total revenue in billions of Euros	**126,875**	**159,337**	**192,676**	**197,007**	**202,458**	**213,292**
Automotive sector revenues						
in billions of Euros	112,806	142,092	172,822	175,003	177,538	183,936
profit before tax	6,189	9,973	9,913	9,807	12,829	−3,634
% return on revenue	**5.48**	**7.01**	**5.73**	**5.6**	**7.22**	**−1.97**
Financial sector revenues						
in billions of Euros	14,069	17,244	19,854	22,004	24,920	29,357
profit before tax	0,952	1,298	1,585	1,863	1,965	2,333
% return on revenue	**6.76**	**7.52**	**7.98**	**8.46**	**8.06**	**7.94**

Source: Volkswagen Annual Report 2015, p.110; 2014, p.23; 2013, p.106; 2012, p.105; 2011, p.111.

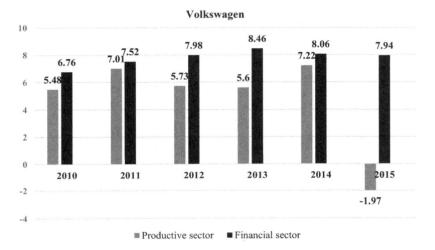

Figure 2.5 Comparison between the sources of profitability in % – Volkswagen
Source: authors, based on the automaker's annual reports.

Table 2.12 shows the participation that each division of the Volkswagen automaker had in the composition of profits from 2000 to 2015.

We can see that there have been great gaps in the profitability of the productive sector. Our series starts in 2000, with a proportion of 85% participation for the productive sector and 15% participation of the financial sector. In 2003, this proportion changes to 49% to 51% for the financial sector, and in the same way in 2004, which raised the proportion of contribution from the financial sector to 56% of the total, leaving 44% contribution to the automotive sector. The peak of the contribution of the automotive sector was in 2011, with 89% contribution, against only 11% contribution of the financial sector.

However, one piece of data calls our attention, which is the consistency of growth of the financial sector's contribution, in absolute terms. It started with just over €500 million in 2000 and reached €2.2 billion in 2015 that is more than a 400% growth. There was only a setback from 2008 to 2009, when the contribution of the financial sector fell from €905 million to €591 million. However, in the following year, it already returned to a contribution in absolute numbers of €952 million in 2010.

The contributions of the automotive sector, on the other hand, are erratic and highly subject to fluctuations in demand. If we take the

Table 2.12 Volkswagen's contribution by sector

	Contribution of VW Automotive in billions of euros	%	Contribution of VW Financial in billions of euros	%
2000	3,288	85	0,551	15
2001	4,625	89	0,552	11
2002	4,040	85	0,721	15
2003	0,886	49	0,894	51
2004	0,715	44	0,927	56
2005	1,859	67	0,933	33
2006	1,166	59	0,843	41
2007	5,194	85	0,957	15
2008	5,428	86	0,905	14
2009	1,264	69	0,591	31
2010	6,189	87	0,952	13
2011	9,973	89	1,298	11
2012	9,913	87	1,585	13
2013	9,807	84	1,863	16
2014	10,780	85	1,917	15
2015	−3,634	0	2,233	100

Source: Volkswagen Annual Reports 2000 to 2015. Income Statement by Division. Available at www.vw.com

series from 2000 to 2015, as shown in Table 2.12, we see that the sector's contribution went from €3 billion in 2000 to €4 billion in 2001, falling to €715 million in 2004, €1.1 billion in 2006. Then, it rose gradually and reached €10 billion in 2014, and fell to a loss of €3.6 billion in 2015, being helped by the financial sector, which profited €2.2 billion.

The consistency of the financial sector's contribution to Volkswagen's business is an indication that financialisation, in this analysis category, is growing, and financial activities are increasingly considered to be very important for the automaker's success.

3 Shareholding composition

This financialisation indicator reflects the volume of participation by groups of institutional investors in the largest automobile manufacturers. Asset management funds are predominantly based in the United States, rising from 41.26% of total assets under management in 2008 to 51.73% in 2018. In the 2010s, there was a large increase in the participation of the United States, Canada, China and Australia in asset managers, while there was a decrease in these managers in Japan (from 8.04% in 2008 to 4.92% of the total in 2018) and in some countries, such as the United Kingdom, which saw its representation of asset managers worldwide fall from 10.5% in 2008 to 7.58% in 2018 (Willis Towers Watson, 2019, p.12). This is a process of reconcentrating capital in large North American groups as we will see in this work.

Passive investment funds have dominated the American corporate landscape since 2007, and control assets in the order of trillions of dollars (Fichtner et al. 2017). The largest one, BlackRock, Inc., based in New York, invested in 4,837 different stocks in 2017. Its main investments were in Technology (21.94%), health (12.92%) and industry (11.02%) (Nasdaq, 2018). As of 30 June 2019, BlackRock's assets under management totalled US$6.84 trillion in shares, fixed income, cash management, alternative investments, real estate and consulting strategies. The fund has 13,000 employees and has offices in 30 countries (BlackRock, 2019).

Second among the largest financial groups is the Vanguard Group, Inc., based in Valley Forge, Pennsylvania. It started operations in 1975 and collected assets under management worth US$6.2 trillion on 31 January 2020. It has 17,600 employees and offices in 15 countries, with about 190 funds in the United States (including portfolios variable annuities) and about 230 additional funds in markets outside the United States. It aggregates more than 30 million investors, in about 170 countries (Vanguard, 2020). In 2017, it invested in 4,025 different shares

DOI: 10.4324/9781003161141-3

and different branches of the economy. Technology (21.29%) and financial services (21.23%) were the biggest sectors in which this giant bet its chips. Health (12.15%), industry (11.63%) and energy (5.62%) were also part of its portfolio. Vanguard is the largest shareholder in Apple, Microsoft, Amazon, Alphabet, JPMorgan, Exxon Mobil, and also Ford and GM (Nasdaq, 2018).

Another giant investor is State Street Corporation. Headquartered in Boston, Massachusetts, the group had assets under management of US$2.5 trillion in 2018 (Willis Towers Watson, 2019, p.38), ranking third among the top investment fund managers. State Street Corp. invested in 3,616 shares, mainly divided into technology (20.55%), financial services (20.24%), industries (12.83%) and health (12.82%), reaching a total of two-thirds of all investments in these four main sectors of the economy.

We describe only the three main North American investment funds, also known as The Big Three (Fichtner et al., 2017), and we will now see what participation they and other large groups hold in the five largest automotive companies worldwide.

Ford

With approximately 4 billion shares launched on the financial market, on 6 August 2015, Ford owned 41.25% of non-institutional shares, that is, individuals and 58.75% of institutional shares, held by corporations and investment groups that practically dominate its composition. For this study, we will not distinguish common from preferred shares. This will be left for further analysis.

Institutional shareholders numbered 1,127 and held 2,289,327,416 shares, valued at US$33.882 billion. However, only the five largest shareholders controlled 34% of institutional shares. They are the Vanguard Group, Inc., with 9.44%, Evercore Trust Company, NA, with 9.4%, State Street Corp, with 6.54%, Blackrock Institutional Trust Company, NA, with 4.27% and Barrow Hanley Mewhinney & Strauss LLC, responsible for 3.57%. These are all gigantic financial service corporations (Nasdaq, 2015a).

If we add five more major shareholders, Wellington Management Group LLP, Fidelity Management and Research – FMR LLC, Allianz Asset Management AG, Loomis Sayles & Company LP and Northern Trust Corporation, they control amounts to no less than 45% of the shares. In other words, Ford's ten largest shareholders are financial groups that alone held more than 1 billion shares valued at US$15.682 billion (Nasdaq, 2015a).

Table 3.1 Largest Ford shareholders – 6 August 2015

Investor	Shares	%	Value in US$	%
Vanguard Group, Inc.	219,797,431	9.44	3,110,134,000	9.45
Evercore Trust Company, NA	218,924,994	9.40	3,097,789,000	9.41
State Street Corp	152,403,918	6.54	2,156,515,000	6.55
Blackrock Institutional Trust Company, NA	99,585,663	4.27	1,409,137,000	4.28
Barrow Hanley Mewhinney & Strauss LLC	83,122,740	3.57	1,176,187,000	3.58
Wellington Management Group LLP	76,998,498	3.30	1,089,529,000	3.31
Franklin Resources, Inc.	73,899,080	3.17	1,045,672,000	3.18
Allianz Asset Management AG	49,559,296	2.12	701,264,000	2.13
Loomis Sayles & Co LP	47,463,547	2.03	671,609,000	2.03
Northern Trust Corp	43,793,391	1.88	619,676,000	1.89
Bank of America Corp/DE	43,277,751	1.85	612,380,000	1.86
JPMorgan Chase & Co	42,445,613	1.82	600,605,000	1.83
Blackrock Fund Advisors	40,895,998	1.75	578,678,000	1.76
The Bank of New York Mellon Corp	38,807,668	1.66	549,129,000	1.67
FMR LLC	32,808,857	1.40	464,245,000	1.41
Total of the 15 largest	**1,263,784,445**	**54.28%**	**17,882,549,000**	**54.33%**

Source: Nasdaq, 2015a.

When we expand this group to the fifteen largest shareholders, leaving more than one thousand investors behind, control reaches 54%, with shares valued at more than US$17 billion. That is, 1.3% of the shareholders concentrated more than half of the values and shares. Although there is a belief that we would be in a shareholder democracy, with thousands of small and medium shareholders dispersed in a competitive environment, the fact is that few groups hold the majority of the company's share control, define their investment strategies, divestment, salaries, jobs, hiring or firing, among other management decisions that depend on the approval of these institutional investors.

Table 3.1 shows Ford's fifteen largest shareholders, all large economic groups and funds that diversify its capital, mixing financial activities with investments in manufacturing companies.

As we can see, Ford's main investors are groups of passive investment funds, and the aforementioned Big Three, Vanguard Group, BlackRock and State Street Corp can be highlighted, increasingly present around the world, participating in the stock rights of thousands

Table 3.2 Ford's largest mutual funds

Funds	30 March 2016 to 29 June 2016			
	Shares	*%*	*Value in US$*	*%*
Vanguard Total Stock Market Index Fund	75,112,631	1.92	1,014,020,518	1.92
Franklin Custodian Funds-Income Fund	62,841,458	1.61	848,359,683	1.61
Vanguard/Wellington Fund, Inc.	52,143,870	1.34	703,420,806	1.34
Vanguard 500 Index Fund	49,171,420	1.26	663,814,170	1.26
Vanguard/Windsor II	46,570,854	1.19	631,500,780	1.19
Vanguard Institutional Index Fund-Institutional Index Fund	43,110,546	1.10	581,992,371	1.10
SPDR S&P 500 ETF Trust	38,712,144	0.99	486,611,650	0.99
Loomis Sayles Bond Fund	21,480,222	0.55	289,982,997	0.55
Fidelity 500 Index Fund	20,613,125	0.53	259,106,981	0.53
Select Sector SPDR Fund-Consumer Discretionary	16,881,796	0.43	212,204,175	0.43
Total	**426,638,066**	**10.92**	**5,691,014,131**	**10.92**

Source: Yahoo Finance, 2016a.

of companies. As they are shareholders in various sectors, this has led to a reconcentration of ownership in a few hands (Davis, 2009) and the creation of immense investment groups, with great power of decision.

Table 3.2 shows the ten largest mutual funds that have invested in Ford. Of the ten largest, five are directly linked to the Vanguard Group and the others are managed by billionaire financial entities and linked to indexes such as S&P, for example. Together, they hold more than 400 million shares, at a value that exceeds US$5 billion.

If we add the 54.28% belonging to the fifteen largest shareholders to the 10.92% of the ten largest mutual funds, then we will have 65.2% that is held by only 25 investors, undoubtedly a huge concentration of ownership in very few hands. Although there is not a majority shareholder, thousands of independent investors, the meeting of a few shareholders (25) concentrates two-thirds of all shares held by institutional investors.

The groups that make up the two lists above do not participate in direct control of the Ford automaker, appointing members to its Board, but exercise their decisions through the annual general meeting, which elects the board of directors and determines the compensation policy for executives, the payment of dividends to shareholders, among other decisions. It is at this annual meeting that they decide the company's strategy for the following year, according to the number of shares they own and their proportion of voting rights. The members of the Board of Directors, however, maintain a close relationship with investors, having even gone through the world of finance, as we will see later in the chapter that deals with the origin of company directors.

General Motors

With more than one and a half billion shares outstanding, General Motors has mostly institutional shareholders. Large investment funds, as well as banks and insurance companies, held 74.56% of the outstanding shares in 2016. Non-institutional shareholders, small investors and individuals, accounted for the remaining 25.44% of the shares. The total value of GM's outstanding shares exceeded US$33 billion, with the share price closing at US$28.78 on Friday afternoon, 19 February 2016 (see Table 3.3).

Even more than Ford, which held 58.75% of the shares in the hands of institutional shareholders, as we saw in the previous case, GM has a degree of concentration of few and large investors that makes its governance subject to the control of a few and billionaire economic groups that have a significant, if not majority, share in financial services. They have a great influence on Board decisions at the North American automaker. Table 3.4 shows the main shareholders, the number of shares they held, the percentage of the total and the estimated value that their shares reached in the market.

As we have seen, General Motors' fifteen largest shareholders are large financial groups and investment funds. As with Ford, some giants appear again. Vanguard Group, State Street Corp., BlackRock, Inc., Bank of America, among others, are also the main shareholders of GM.

Table 3.3 Institutional and non-institutional shareholders – GM, 19 February 2016

Institutional shareholders	74.56%
Non-institutional shareholders	25.44%
Total Institutional shareholders	1,005
Total Institutional shares	1,151,545,593
Total outstanding shares	1,544,000,000
Total value of shares – in US$	33,429,368,565

Source: Nasdaq, 2016b.

Table 3.4 Largest General Motors shareholders – 19 February 2016

Investor	Shares	%	Value in US$	%
Vanguard Group, Inc.	82,980,517	7.21	2,408,924,000	7.20
Harris Associates LP	81,083,512	7.04	2,353,854,000	7.04
State Street Corporation	56,735,840	4.93	1,647,041,000	4.93
Berkshire Hathaway, Inc.	50,000,000	4.34	1,451,500,000	4.34
JPMorgan Chase & Company	49,269,836	4.28	1,430,303,000	4.28
FMR, LLC	43,146,784	3.74	1,252,551,000	3.74
BlackRock Institutional Trust Company, NA	37,503,237	3.25	1,088,719,000	3.25
Capital Research Global Investors	36,572,606	3.17	1,061,703,000	3.17
Franklin Resources, Inc.	35,287,118	3.06	1,024,385,000	3.06
Capital World Investors	22,168,192	1.92	643,543,000	1.92
Bank of America Corp/DE	20,829,113	1.81	604,669,000	1.81
Invesco LTD	18,887,106	1.64	548,293,000	1.64
Blackrock Fund Advisors	16,721,224	1.45	485,417,000	1.45
Northern Trust Corp.	15,528,658	1.35	450,797,000	1.35
Janus Capital Management LLC	14,112,914	1.22	409,698,000	1.22
Total of 15 largest	**580,826,657**	**50.41**	**16,861,397,000**	**50.41**

Source: Nasdaq, 2016b.

These 15 largest shareholders together held 50.41% of the institutional shares, which totalled US$ 16.8 billion, half of the total value of the company's shares, which was US$33.4 billion in 2016. This gives an enormous power of decision in the strategies defined by the company. The Vanguard Group alone held 7.21% of the shares, with a value of almost US$2.5 billion. At Ford, the same Vanguard Group had around US$3 billion in 2016 with more than 200 million shares, almost 10% stake. Moreover, these numbers have grown even more. The Vanguard Group held 94 million shares in General Motors in 2020, at a value of US$4.188 billion, that is, 8.35% of the total. BlackRock, which was the seventh-largest shareholder in 2016, became the first in 2020, jumping from 37 million shares to 106 million, almost tripling its presence and adding a 9.41% share of the company (Nasdaq, 2020a).

In addition to this North American giant, other investment funds also participate in the management of General Motors. State Street Corp is one of them. As already mentioned in the case of Ford, this is a diversified group, with 19.05% of shares in the services sector, 17.57% in the financial sector, 16.42% in the technology sector and 11.79% in the health services. It also invests in energy (6.9%), capital goods (6.58%) and basic materials (3.25%) (Nasdaq, 2016a).

Finally, we draw your attention to the Bank of America and Berkshire Hathaway. The Bank of America held more than 20 million shares in General Motors and is one of the largest North American banks. Its market capitalisation was estimated at US$382.9 billion on 25 April 2016, and its investment portfolio amounted to 6,274 positions, that is, it invested in more than six thousand companies. Its main business, despite diversification, is the financial sector, to which it dedicates 43.99% of its investments. Services (13.11%), technology (10.05%) and health (7.06%) are also sectors in which the bank invests (Nasdaq, 2016a).

Berkshire Hathaway is a US investment fund based in Omaha, Nebraska, with an estimated market capitalisation of US$133 billion. It is led by billionaire Warren Buffett, who has a net worth estimated at US$65.9 billion (Kroll, 2016). It held 50 million shares of General Motors at an amount, on April 26, 2016, of US$1.597 billion. It is a financial group that does not diversify its investments very much, compared to the groups described above, as it has had only 48 different roles in its investment portfolio. Finance (32.28%) was its main activity. Although it also invests heavily in companies such as Kraft Heinz (US$25.6 billion), Wells Fargo (US$24.2 billion) and Coca Cola (US$17.8 billion), it is the largest shareholder in these three famous companies (Nasdaq, 2016a)

There are also mutual funds maintained by financial groups. At General Motors, the top ten in 2016 were those shown in Table 3.5.

Note that mutual funds are also held by financial institutions and at least three of these funds are managed by the Vanguard Group. Others, such as SPDR S&P 500 ETF Trust, JPMorgan, Fidelity 500 Index Fund, held more than 100 million shares of General Motors, at a value of US$4.3 billion on 14 September 2016. In this indicator, General Motors repeats the Ford standard, with characteristics typical of companies in the United States, with a strong presence and influence of passive, active, mutual, pension funds on their property rights. A very different picture than that of Hyundai, for example, which we will see in the next case.

Hyundai

Hyundai's shareholding composition is somewhat different from that of North American automakers. While at Ford and General Motors there are billions of shares issued on the market, with a high degree of dispersion (although few shareholders hold significant shares of participation), at Hyundai around 280 million shares were outstanding at the end of 2015. The common shares were over 220 million and preferred shares just over 65 million (see Table 3.6).

Table 3.5 General Motors' largest mutual funds

	Ten largest mutual funds from 30 March to 29 June 2016			
	Shares	*%*	*Value in US$*	*%*
Vanguard Total Stock Market Index Fund	26,766,792	1.74	841,280,272	1.74
Vanguard 500 Index Fund	17,715,770	1.15	556,806,651	1.15
Investment Company of America	16,370,309	1.06	463,279,728	1.06
Vanguard Institutional Index Fund-Institutional Index Fund	15,522,805	1.01	487,881,761	1.01
Income Fund of America, Inc	15,248,112	0.99	431,521,554	0.99
SPDR S&P 500 ETF Trust	13,892,569	0.90	393,159,688	0.90
Janus Twenty Fund	11,256,328	0.73	318,554,071	0.73
Franklin Custodian Funds-Income Fund	10,621,840	0.69	333,844,431	0.69
JPMorgan US Large Cap Core Plus Fund	9,338,149	0.61	264,269,607	0.61
Fidelity 500 Index Fund	7,402,378	0.48	209,487,289	0.48
Total	**144,135,052**	**9.36**	**4,300,085,052**	**9.36**

Source: Yahoo Finance, 2016b.

Table 3.6 Hyundai shares by type

31 December 2015	
Common shares	220,276,479
Preferential shares	65,202,146
Treasury shares	16,812,453
Total shares	302,291,078

Source: Hyundai Motor Company, 2016b.

When we look at Hyundai's largest shareholders, we see a picture that is also different from that of the United States. Although there are institutional investors who hold millions of shares, most of them were in the hands of some of the companies in the conglomerate, such as Hyundai Mobis Co., which alone holds more than 45 million shares, or 20.8% of the total, at one worth more than US$5 billion. After that comes South Korea's National Pension Service, with more than 16 million shares, 7.42%. The third is Hyundai Motor Co. Ltd, with more than 13 million shares and 6% of the total. President Mong-Koo Chung was the fourth largest shareholder, with 5.17%, valued at almost US$1.5 billion. Vice President Eui-Sun Chung was the fifth largest shareholder, with more than 5 million shares, or 2.28%.

Only then do we see the big Western institutional investors who also participate in Ford and GM, as is the case with Vanguard Group and BlackRock Fund advisors. This situation refers to the fact that financialisation at Hyundai seems to be late concerning its North American counterparts, as we will see throughout this work. But even so, we can see that the ten largest shareholders concentrate almost 50% of all shares and, with that, repeat the performance of their competitors Ford and GM, whose largest shareholders also concentrate just over half of all shares. Table 3.7 shows these data.

These figures have hardly changed until today, December 2020, with only a few changes in the order of shareholders, and growth in South Korea's National Pension Service to 10.8% of the shares. Vanguard Group, Inc. rose to a 1.91% stake, Norges Bank Investment Management now has 1.29% of the shares, Thornburg Investment Management, Inc. has 1.09%, Capital Research & Management Co. (World Investors) has 1.01%, in addition to Artisan Partners LP, with 0.92% of the automaker's shares.

Table 3.7 Largest shareholders of Hyundai – 2015

	Ten largest shareholders		
	Shares	*%*	*Value in US$*
Hyundai Mobis Co. Ltd.	45,782,023	20.8	5,783,185,145.36
National Pension Service of Korea	16,344,357	7.42	2,064,619,176.24
Hyundai Motor Co. Ltd.	13,222,314	6.00	1,670,242,704.48
Mong Koo Chung	11,395,859	5.17	1,439,524,908.88
Eui Sun Chung	5,017,145	2.28	633,765,756.40
Capital Research & Management Co. (World Investors)	4,128,447	1.87	521,505,425.04
Templeton Global Advisors Ltd.	4,043,285	1.84	510,747,761.20
The Vanguard Group, Inc.	2,837,713	1.29	358,459,906.16
BlackRock Fund Advisors	2,615,237	1.19	330,356,737.84
Capital Research & Management Co. (Global Investors)	2,328,061	1.06	294,080,665.52
Total	**107,714,441**	**48.92**	**13,606,488,187.12**

Source: Hyundai Motor Company, 2016b; MarketScreener, 2016.

This is a different shareholding composition from North American automakers because there is no predominance of funds and other financial institutions concentrating most of the shares. Only the Pension Fund, with 10.8% and the other investor funds, does not reach more than 30% of the shares in Hyundai, and the other major investors are of the company itself, members of the conglomerate and the owners. Hyundai participates in several holding companies, with different percentages, such as Hyundai Engineering & Construction Co., Ltd, with 20.9%; Hyundai Rotem Company, with 33.8%; Hyundai Autoever Corporation, with 28.5%; Hyundai Glovis Co., Ltd., with 4.88%; Hyundai Wia Corporation, with 25.3%; Hyundai Steel Company, with 6.87% and Korea Shipbuilding & Offshore Engineering Co., Ltd, with 2.31%, among others. It is a typical conglomerate of family origin.

In summary, we can say that Hyundai's shareholding structure is different from that of the North American ones, reflecting its relationship between the state, capital, labour and companies, configuring a still initial financialisation process, with a different dynamic, with less participation and dependence of financial capital on company rights, unlike competitors based in the United States.

Toyota

At Toyota, the shareholding structure is relatively similar to that of the United States. There are more than 3 billion shares issued on the market. However, here there is a difference between Ford and GM. In North America, the number of institutional shareholders in 2015 was around one thousand (1,127 at Ford and 1,155 at GM), while at Toyota there were 613,648 shareholders, showing a degree of much greater dispersion than that of its US competitors, as we can see in Table 3.8.

The shareholding structure, shown in Table 3.9, gives leadership to investors from financial institutions and brokers, which accounted for 31.11% of shareholders in 2014. Afterwards, foreign corporate entities

Table 3.8 Toyota's shares

31 March 2014	
Outstanding shares	3,447,997,492
Treasury shares	278,231,473
Total number of shareholders	613,648
Total value of common shares in yen	397,049,000,000.00

Source: Toyota Annual Report, 2014. Investors, p. 68.

Table 3.9 Ownership structure – Toyota

in %	
Financial Institutions and Brokers	31.11
Foreign and other corporate entities	30.36
Individuals	20.67
Other corporate entities	17.86

Source: Toyota Annual Report, 2014 – Investors, p. 68

represented 30.36%. Individuals make up 20.67% of the shareholders, while other corporate entities hold 17.86% of the shares.

These data reinforce the thesis of financialisation in one of its very important aspects, which is the increasing participation of financial institutions in the management of the business, increasingly making acquisitions of shares and increasing their control over the automaker. Table 3.10 shows the list of the top ten Toyota shareholders in March 2014.

As we can see from Table 3.10, the biggest shareholders are banks. From the ten largest, six are banks. Then, two are insurance companies and a worldwide manufacturer of automotive components (Denso Corporation). In addition to Toyota Industries Corporation, which is the second largest shareholder, but holds only 6.48% of the shares, it has to share decisions with other groups of investors, precisely because it is a minority partner.

In this category that studies the shareholders, we see that Toyota is even more dominated by financial institutions than Ford and GM. Here, in this case, they are dependent on the banks, and much more so than Hyundai. Toyota's financialisation dates back to the 1950s when strikes and serious crises emerged, and it passed its sales on credit to banks, already at that time, in addition to laying off almost 30% of its workforce in 1953 (Elías and Granados 2015, p.6).

That is, the degree of dependence that Toyota has on the banks is old, also different from the financialisation process that occurs in the North American ones, because their institutional investors are the modern passive investment funds, pension funds, among other funds. Banks come in as smaller shareholders, compared to gigantic groups such as Vanguard Group or BlackRock.

We can deduce from these data that up to now at least three different dynamics have been presented in the issue of shareholding composition: the situation of the North American companies, dependent on passive investment funds; that of Hyundai, a family-type conglomerate with

Table 3.10 Largest Toyota shareholders

	Ten largest shareholders – 31 March 2014		
	Shares	*%*	*Value in US$*
Japan Trustee Services Bank, Ltd.	331,408,000	9.61	20,215,888,000
Toyota Industries Corporation	223,515,000	6.48	13,634,415,000
The Master Trust Bank of Japan, Ltd.	181,754,000	5.27	11,086,994,000
State Street Bank and Trust Company (Standing proxy: Settlement & Clearing Service Division, Mizuho Bank, Ltd.)	128,118,000	3.71	7,815,198,000
Nippon Life Insurance Company	122,323,000	3.54	7,461,703,000
The Bank of New York Mellon as Depositary Bank for Depositary Receipt Holders	83,412,000	2.41	5,088,132,000
Trust & Custody Services Bank, Ltd.	70,824,000	2.05	4,320,264,000
Denso Corporation	69,533,000	2.01	4,241,513,000
Mitsui Sumitomo Insurance Company, Limited	66,063,000	1.91	4,029,843,000
State Street Bank and Trust Company (Standing proxy: The Hong Kong and Shanghai Banking Corporation Limited, Tokyo Branch)	55,260,000	1.60	3,370,860,000
Total	**1,332,210,000**	**38.63**	**81,264,810,000**

Source: Toyota Annual Report, 2014 – Investors, p. 68.

little dependence on financial institutions; and Toyota's dynamics, more dependent on banks than investment funds. Volkswagen will present yet another dynamic, as we will see below.

Volkswagen

In 2005, Porsche acquired 18.53% of Volkswagen's share control. In 2015, it held 30.8% of the subscribed capital and 52.2% in the distribution of voting rights. Foreign institutional investors represented 21.1% of the capital and no percentage of the voting rights. Qatar Holding held 14.6% of the control and 17% of the voting rights. The state of Lower Saxony brings together 11.8% of the subscribed capital and 20% of the voting rights. Private shareholders held 19.4% in 2015 and 10.8% of the voting rights. Table 3.11 shows this distribution.

Table 3.11 Largest Volkswagen shareholders

	In % of subscribed capital 2015	In distribution of voting rights % 2015
Porsche Automobil Holding SE, Stuttgart	30.8	52.2
Foreign Institutional Investors	21.1	0
Qatar Holding LLC	14.6	17
Lower Saxony State, Hanover	11.8	20
Private Shareholders/Others	19.4	10.8
German Institutional Investors	2.3	0

Source: Volkswagen AG, 2015b.

German institutional investors held only 2.3% of the capital and no voting rights. In 2008, the VW Group increased its stake in Scania to 68.6% of the voting rights, becoming the majority shareholder. In 2011, Volkswagen increased its stake in MAN to 55.9% of the shares, also becoming a majority shareholder.

Also different from that of the automakers Ford, GM and Toyota, Volkswagen has a concentration of both subscribed capital and voting rights in the hands of Porsche and the Lower Saxony government, that is, in the hands of a German industrial company and a state of the German federation, whose total share of subscribed capital reached 42.6% and voting rights exceed 72%. Very different from the North American automakers and Japan's Toyota, which have among their major shareholders large banks and financial institutions, at Volkswagen the public interest of the state and a large automotive industry has great weight in decisions. Although this fact did not prevent the distribution of dividends to shareholders from reaching 99.2% of net income in 2012, as we will see later. Here we can also talk about a different dynamic in the case of financialisation at Volkswagen. The participation of foreign institutional investors, private shareholders and German institutional investors, together with 42.8% of the subscribed capital in 2015, resulted in 10.8% of the voting rights, only by private shareholders, leaving institutional investors, both German and foreign, without any voting rights. It is a very peculiar form of participation, given that three large groups of investors have very little share of decision-making power, in a demonstration of the corporate environment strongly influenced by the German state and its economic leadership. We could say that the classification of a coordinated market economy, to qualify German capitalism, where there is an extensive legal framework of regulations and prohibitions, participation and decision-making power in companies would be correct when we analyse the shareholding composition at Volkswagen.

4 Shareholders' acquisitions

The acquisitions of shares that groups of investors carry out in companies in general, and in automakers in particular, are one of the results of the financialisation process, whereby more and more financial institutions are participating in companies not as usual creditors, but as owners of property rights through shares on stock exchanges. This evolution from the debt-to-equity phase can be considered as one of the most striking features of the financialisation process.

Ford

The acquisitions that the financial groups carry out in Ford's shares highlight the policy of the passive funds and especially the banks to increase their possessions and hence their control in the companies' decisions.

Equity movements have been responsible for expanding the participation of banks and financial corporations. In 2015, the Vanguard Group, Inc. acquired more than 12 million shares, now holding 214 million units and increasing its participation by 6.44%.

More aggressive were banks, such as the Bank of America, which acquired 13.5 million shares, increasing its shareholding by 63.41%. JPMorgan Chase & Co. bought more than 8 million shares, increasing its stake in Ford shares by 66.87%. Goldman Sachs Group, Inc. also bought nearly 7 million shares, expanding its stake by 46.83% (Nasdaq, 2015a).

In addition to these extensions that the banks made, other groups were added to Ford's share acquisitions. The biggest stock buyers in 2015 were mainly powerful financial groups, such as Anchor Bolt Capital, LP, which bought more than 8 million shares with a US$117 million injection of capital into the automaker. Other investment funds also participated in Ford's equity acquisitions, such as Dimensional Fund

DOI: 10.4324/9781003161141-4

Table 4.1 Largest stock acquisitions at Ford – 2015

	Shares acquired	In US$
Bank of America Corp/DE	13,454,488	199,530,057.04
Vanguard Group, Inc.	12,984,030	192,553,164.09
Anchor Bolt Capital, LP	8,140,961	117,718,296.06
JPMorgan Chase & Co.	8,004,489	115,744,910.94
Dimensional Fund Advisors LP	7,495,486	111,158,057.38
Goldman Sachs Group, Inc.	6,962,475	103,253,504.25
Hosking Partners LLP	1,456,403	20,608,000.00
Mount Lucas Management LP	1,148,368	16,249,000.00
Artemis Investment Management LLP	1,071,900	15,167,000.00
Profit Investment Management, LLC	789,576	11,173,000.00
Total	61,508,176	903,154,989.76

Source: Nasdaq, 2016c.

Advisors LP, Mount Lucas Management LP, Hosking Partners LLP, Artemis Investment Management LLP, which together acquired more than 10 million shares, bringing the company nearly US$200 million in capital. Altogether, the ten largest financial groups acquired more than 60 million shares, investing an amount of almost US$1 billion in the automaker (Nasdaq, 2015a).

Table 4.1 shows the ten largest groups that acquired Ford shares. This control of the automaker by banks and passive funds, among others, dictates the entire line of the decisions taken by the manufacturer.

This trend observed in 2015 is repeated today. With 1,199 institutional shareholders in late 2020, a total of 425 bought shares, around 128 million shares, while 553 shareholders sold shares, but only 77 million units. Only the top ten concentrated largely on stock purchases. In other words, there is little share dispersion even in the purchasing process, with few shareholders buying millions of shares. Table 4.2 shows the largest shares acquisitions in 2020.

From the 425 shareholders who purchased shares on 30 September 2020 (US$6.59 per share), out of a total of 128 million shares, only ten shareholders purchased nearly 37 million shares or 28.83% of the total purchased. In other words, ten shareholders represent 2.35% of the 425 that bought shares, but that 2.35% bought 28.83% of the total shares, which proves our thesis that there is an increasing shareholder concentration in North American automakers Ford and General Motors, held by large passive, mutual, pension and bank investment funds, leaving little space for small shareholders, who are dispersed and pooling few resources.

Table 4.2 Largest stock acquisitions at Ford – 30 September 2020

	Shares acquired	In US$
Arrowstreet Capital, Limited Partnership	15,036,764	99,092,274.76
BlackRock, Inc.	7,094,408	46,752,148.72
Morgan Stanley	6,959,199	45,861,121.41
Geode Capital Management, LLC	2,293,865	15,116,570.35
Nuveen Asset Management, LLC	2,175,449	14,336,208.91
Bank of New York Mellon Corp	1,335,226	8,799,139.34
UBS Asset Management Americas, Inc.	1,317,723	8,683,794.57
State Street Corp.	450,002	2,965,513.18
Northern Trust Corp.	127,124	837,747.16
Bank of America Corp/DE	122,866	809,686.94
Total	36,912,626	243,254,205.34

Source: Nasdaq, 2020b.

General Motors

The acquisitions made in GM's shares also resemble Ford's acquisition movements. Table 4.3 shows the ten largest acquisitions of shares by financial groups and their market value.

The top ten groups acquired 44 million shares at a value of US$1.5 billion. All are financial groups, banks, insurance companies and passive investment funds. At the top of the list is the German group Allianz Asset Management, which acquired more than 11 million shares and advanced almost US$400 million to GM's coffers. Headquartered in Munich, Germany, this group had US$2.2 trillion in assets under management in 2018 and invested in 1,889 different papers and shares. Similar to the other major shareholders, their investments are concentrated on finance (22.9%), technology (18.76%), services (16.94%) and health (10.64%). Their preferences are similar to those of other financial groups when investing: Apple, Microsoft, Wells Fargo, JPMorgan Chase and AT&T top their investment list (Nasdaq, 2016b).

Second in the acquisitions is another North American giant FMR LLC, Fidelity Management and Research LLC, which acquired more than nine million shares, for a value of US$329 million. This group had US$2.4 trillion in assets under management in 2018 and has a large part of its investments in technology (21.05%), followed by the finance sector (18.63), services (17.82%) and health (13.49%). Its investments are distributed in 2,723 positions and its main roles are Apple, Facebook, Alphabet, Amazon, Visa, Microsoft and JPMorgan Chase (Nasdaq, 2016b).

Table 4.3 Largest stock acquisitions at General Motors

	Ten largest acquisitions – 2015 – share price US$35	
	Shares acquired	In US$
Allianz Asset Management AG	11,218,199	394,744,000.00
FMR LLC	9,405,214	329,182,490.00
Wellington Management Group LLC	7,371,113	257,988,955.00
AQR Capital Management LLC	3,445,667	120,598,345.00
UBS Group AG	2,722,269	95,279,415.00
Wells Fargo & Company/MN	2,696,904	94,391,640.00
Artemis Investment Management LLP	2,383,873	83,435,555.00
HSBC Holdings PLC	1,955,896	68,456,360.00
Arrowstreet Capital Limited Partnership	1,596,800	55,880,000.00
Two Sigma Investments	1,570,610	54,971,350.00
Total	44,366,545	1,554,928,110.00

Source: Nasdaq, 2015b.

When we survey every major GM shareholder, we see a huge resemblance to Ford investors. Perhaps because both are North American companies and most investors are also, and because the profit from financial activities proportionally is greater than the profit from productive activities, it is a great advantage to invest in this increasingly financialised industrial sector as well.

Hyundai

For transparency issues that have not been resolved for a long time, Hyundai does not pay much attention to data centralisation. We were unable to systematically find the main groups that acquired shares in the South Korean automaker in 2016, neither on the company's websites nor on other more specialised ones. However, the data we were able to find refers to two groups of investors, which acquired a few thousand shares in 2016. They are Perennial Investment Partners Ltd, which bought 79,615 shares of the automaker and Antipodes Partners Limited, which acquired 17,900 shares of Hyundai. In other words, even having little data to collect, those we managed to get help confirm our initial concern: more and more financial groups are acquiring shares in car manufacturers around the world, advancing in their property rights and in the most important decisions of their management.

Table 4.4 Largest Hyundai shareholders in KR 7005381009 shares

Investor	Number of shares	% of total
National Pension Service of Korea	5,338,841	21.9
Hyundai Motor Company	2,186,993	8.98
Skagen AS (Investment Management)	702,782	2.89
The Vanguard Group, Inc.	451,327	1.85
Causeway Capital Management LLC	239,027	0.98
The Caisse de dépôt et placement du Québec	185,326	0.76
Weiss Asset Management LP	167,225	0.69
Value Partners Ltd.	166,619	0.68
BlackRock Advisors (UK) Ltd.	152,120	0.62
Robeco Institutional Asset Management BV	149,433	0.61

Source: MarketScreener, 2016.

This can be seen better now. In a subsequent survey, based on the data found on the marketscreener.com website, we can see that in 2020 the most recent shareholders of Hyundai, which hold other types of shares, were as follows (see Table 4.4).

The shareholders shown in Table 4.4 are very similar to the main shareholders discussed in the previous chapter. Here we have the South Korean pension fund as the largest, followed by the company itself, Hyundai Motor Company and far behind come the foreign investment funds, with stakes ranging from 0.61% to 2.89%. Again, we look at the Vanguard Group and BlackRock, Inc. on the top ten list, however, with much lower percentages than they held at Ford and General Motors.

Following the shares listed on the South Korea stock exchange, we see more groups of institutional investors holding larger shares, but still much smaller than the groups of the conglomerate itself and the South Korean national pension fund, previously seen in the other tables (see Table 4.5).

The bulk of the shares in this modality remain with the company, with the investment funds holding a small share of the shares, with the first ten accounting for just over 25% of the total. However, this type of share is numerically small, and the vast majority is held by the companies presented in the previous chapter. Table 4.6 shows another modality of shares, also in an even smaller number.

Finally, we see the shares quoted in the United States, in a number that approaches 2 million shares, small compared to the almost 280 million total shares launched by Hyundai and which are held by groups belonging to the family-type conglomerate.

Table 4.5 Largest Hyundai shareholders in KR 7005382007 shares

Investor	Number of shares	% of total
Fidelity Management & Research Co. LLC	1,730,809	4.74
Invesco Asset Management Ltd.	1,609,759	4.41
Hyundai Motor Company	1,353,570	3.71
The Vanguard Group, Inc.	1,180,078	3.23
Capital Research & Management Co. (Global Investors)	943,537	2.59
BlackRock Fund Advisors	855,317	2.34
Schroder Investment Management Ltd.	683,902	1.87
Fiduciary Management, Inc.	605,400	1.66
Skagen AS (Investment Management)	505,927	1.39
Kopernik Global Investors LLC	459,018	1.13

Source: MarketScreener, 2016.

Table 4.6 Largest Hyundai shareholders in KR 7005383005 shares

Investor	Number of shares	% of total
Hyundai Motor Company	48,574	2.00
Invesco Canada Ltd.	17,201	0.71
Renta 4 Gestora SGIIC SA	10,751	0.44
Amiral Gestion SA	10,250	0.42
Invesco Advisers, Inc.	8,674	0.36
Arrowstreet Capital LP	3,820	0.16
FIL Investment Advisors (UK) Ltd.	2,930	0.12
CATAM Asset Management AG	1,925	0.079
Wellington Management Co. LLP	1,409	0.058
Value Partners Ltd.	1,297	0.053

Source: MarketScreener, 2016.

This opening of shares in the United States is more symbolic; it has little weight on the company's shares since the number of shares held is very small concerning the total, but it is a step towards expanding the participation of future institutional investors in the company's stock rights.

Table 4.7 shows the largest shareholders in the United States and they are all large groups of institutional investors, although they hold small amounts of shares and percentage of participation.

In summary, we can deduce from these data that the largest shareholders, in all types of shares listed in different exchanges (and that they are the ones who buy and sell these shares) are members of the

Table 4.7 Largest Hyundai shareholders (USA) – 2020

Investor	Number of shares	% of total
BlackRock Fund Advisors	438,378	0.90
Allianz Global Investors U.S. LLC	101,700	0.21
Charles Schwab Investment Management, Inc.	69,893	0.14
City National Rochdale LLC	50,900	0.10
Operadora Valmex de Fondos de Inversión SA de CV	40,098	0.082
Aberdeen Asset Managers Ltd.	40,000	0.082
Nomura Asset Management USA, Inc.	27,562	0.057
OFFIT Investment Group	25,000	0.051
Schafer Cullen Capital Management, Inc.	17,891	0.037
Popular Gestión Privada SGIIC SA	12,512	0.026

Source: MarketScreener, 2016.

conglomerate itself and that foreign institutional investors, investment funds liabilities and others are still a minority when compared to group companies and proprietary partners, which are still in force at the automaker and have enormous influence and decision-making power.

Toyota

The equity acquisitions further strengthen the participation of financial institutions in the Japanese automaker. The Japan Trustee Services Bank was the largest acquirer of Toyota shares in March 2016. More than 27 million shares were acquired at a market value of more than US$1.6 billion. Denso Corporation, a manufacturer of automotive components, was the only major shareholder that does not come from the direct financial world, and acquired nearly 17 million shares, injecting more than US$1 billion into the company. Third, another bank alone acquired 8.2 million shares, JPMorgan Chase & Company, followed by Toyota Industries itself, which acquired approximately 1 million shares, as we can see in Table 4.8.

In the United States, the Toyota Motor Corporation is listed on the New York Stock Exchange and also on Nasdaq, where it has 367 institutional investors, bringing together 15,939,159 common shares.

Toyota's largest share acquisitions in 2020 at Nasdaq were all from financial institutions, as can be seen in Table 4.9.

One of the largest investment funds, Fidelity Management (FMR LLC), acquired thousands of shares, increasing its stake by 32.13%,

Table 4.8 Largest stock acquisitions at Toyota – Japan, 2016

Investor	Shares	%	Value in US$
Japan Trustee Services Bank, Ltd	27,203,000	0.78	1,659,383,000
Denso Corporation	16,980,000	0.49	1,035,780,000
JPMorgan Chase & Company	8,221,000	0.23	501,481,000
Toyota Industries Corporation	1,000,000	0.02	61,000,000
Total	53,404,000	1.52	3,257,644,000

Source: Toyota Motor Corporation, 2016a.

Table 4.9 Largest stock acquisitions at Toyota – United States – Nasdaq 2020

Investor	Shares	Change (%)
Fisher Asset Management, LLC	213,399	5.55
Susquehanna International Group, LLP	94,207	New
Goldman Sachs Group, Inc.	51,233	9.39
FMR LLC	49,045	32.13
First Trust Advisors LP	38,293	10.61
Morgan Stanley	34,663	15.32
Schafer Cullen Capital Management, Inc.	32,416	9.34
Bank of America Corp/DE	31,493	5.69
Natixis Advisors, LP	12,680	12.15
Martin Investment Management, LLC	10,940	16.25
Envestnet Asset Management, Inc.	10,212	5.99
Wells Fargo & Company/MN	8,987	8.92
Stifel Financial Corp.	2,652	2.65

Source: Nasdaq, 2020c.

accompanied by Morgan Stanley, who increased its stake by 15.32% and Fisher Asset Management, which bought 213 thousand shares of the automaker, increasing its participation by 5.55%. In other words, they are all large groups of institutional investors, reflecting the particularity that occurs in the United States, which is the predominance of modern and powerful passive investment funds, among other asset managers.

Volkswagen

Because of the 2015 emissions scandal involving the company, many shareholders preferred to sell Volkswagen shares. The fall in stock prices, from more than 250.00 euros to less than 90.00 in a few months, scared investors. Even so, private shareholders were the ones that most acquired shares, going from 12.3% of the shares to the control of 19.4% of them. However, their voting rights fell from 12.3% to 10.8%, that is, they were weakened. Porsche Automobil Holding SE, which sold some of its shares, falling from 31.5% of the shares to 30.8%, increased its voting right from 50.7% to 52.2%, or 1.5% of addition. Qatar Holding LLC sold shares and went from 15.4% of controlling interest to 14.6%, remaining with the same 17% voting rights. The same thing happened with the state of Lower Saxony, which reduced its shareholding percentage from 12.4% to 11.8%, but maintained its voting right at 20% of the total.

As of 31 December 2019, the percentage of subscribed capital in the German automaker was as follows: Porsche Automobil Holding SE, with 31.3% of the shares and 53.3% of the voting rights; foreign institutional investors, with 26.3% and no voting rights; Qatar Holding LLC, with 14.6% of the shares and 17% of the voting rights; private shareholders, with 12.9% of the shares and without voting rights; Lower Saxony State, with 11.8% of the shares and 20% of the voting rights, and German institutional investors, with only 3.1% of the shares. That is, little has changed in the shareholding composition and the shareholding acquisitions in the Volkswagen automaker in the last five years since it continues with a shareholding structure with the predominance of the industry and a state of the German federation. Foreign and institutional investors, while holding a significant portion of the shares, have little or no voting rights, except for Qatar Holding. This reflects different governance from the North American companies (Ford and GM) and also from the Japanese Toyota, in which the predominance is given by investment funds and banks, respectively.

5   Origin of the company directors

A constituent aspect of the financialisation process of society is that the main management positions of companies must be filled with professionals who are in tune with the assumptions and needs of finance. According to the "conception of control" approach (Fligstein, 1990), the company's president or director previously had a production-oriented mindset, as something fundamental for business development. Finance was only a means of fostering a productive enterprise. Then came an era of the predominance of sales and marketing strategy, expansion of markets and diversification of products, which put people committed to these sales and marketing strategies in the main command posts. Afterwards, financial strategies gave the primacy of command to individuals from the financial world or whoever passed through financial organisations.

From the point of view of occupying positions in organisations, the financialisation strategy is guided by the preference for professionals with experience in finance, focus on obtaining short-term economic and financial results, use of variable remuneration linked to financial and market performance actions, focus on capital appreciation through financial logic instead of production logic, strengthening the corporate governance structure and using interconnected boards of directors (Fantti and Donadone, 2020, p.4).

And this is what we see in the main automakers worldwide, although here in this financialisation indicator, there are different dynamics in the composition of the personnel who run the companies, depending on the country and the culture in which they are inserted. We will see that at Ford and GM, several directors of the Board of Directors and also several executives have already participated in financial organisations before participating in the command of the automakers. In others, such as Hyundai, Toyota and Volkswagen, the trajectory of managers is different; most of the time there are no managers from the world of finance.

DOI: 10.4324/9781003161141-5

Ford

At Ford, the Board of Directors is made up of the president and heir William Clay Ford Jr. and 14 more directors. At least half of the directors have or have had interests in banks, insurance companies and other financial institutions. That is, more than half of the board is made up of people who are or were part of financial organisations and who bring their beliefs and values shaped by the world of finance into the automaker.

With a team assembled in the image and similarity of the financial market, the ideology of maximising the return to the shareholder becomes natural and free of obstacles. Table 5.1 shows the executives'

Table 5.1 Origin of Ford managers – 2016

Board of Directors	Financial Organisations in which they participate or participated
Kimberly A. Casiano Director	Bank of Scotland – Porto Rico Mutual of America Capital Management LLC
Anthony F. Earley Jr Independent Director	New York Stock Exchange Mutual of America Capital Management LLC Comerica Bank Comerica Incorporated
Edsel B. Ford II Director	Federal Reserve Bank of Chicago
Richard A. Gephardt Director	ACO Investment Group New Cycle Capital LLC Goldman Sachs Pension Practice American Income Life Insurance Company
James P. Hackett Director	Old Kent Financial Corp. Fifth Third Bank Northwestern Mutual Life Insurance Company
James H. Hance Jr Director	Carlyle Group LP Bank of America Corp.
William E. Kennard Director	Grain Capital Staple Street Capital LLC MetLife, Inc. Metropolitan Life Insurance Company
Gerald L. Shaheen Chief of the nominating and governance council	North American Chamber of Commerce AGCO Corp National City Corporation
John Lawson Thornton Director	Barrick Gold Corporation San Shan Capital Partners Laura Ashley Holdings PLC Goldman Sachs Group, Inc.

Source: Ford Motor Company, 2016.

relationships with the financial organisations that participate or participated.

These directors also participate in other boards, constituting an extensive relationship network, which favours the flow of information and gives them enormous power of decision and influence in this complex corporate world that is currently developing.

General Motors

When we look at GM executives, or the vast majority of them, we see executives who have stakes or have had stakes in large companies and large economic groups. Although many of these managers participate in companies in the industrial segment, these firms are owned by gigantic holding companies, which diversify their activities and the financial strategy prevails, as attested by the company's message to shareholders, when calling for the election of officers on 9 June 2015.

To justify the stewardship of Stephen Girsky, the company says that his admission to the board, given his experience as president of a private equity firm, "brings significant expertise in finance, market and risk analysis and business development and restructuring". Regarding Linda Gooden, director since 2015, there is the merit of having experience as a director of other public companies, "particularly in the area of finance, auditing, strategic investments, acquisitions and divestments" (General Motors, 2015b, p.14).

And for the most part, the directors' predicates always refer to the contribution they can make when they perceive their experience in the financial area. In this financialisation indicator, General Motors has a performance similar to that of its competitor Ford, considering what we have already said about the cultural and economic conditions in the United States, which allows for an extremely developed and influential financial market. Table 5.2 shows the participation of GM's directors in large companies, banks and gigantic economic groups.

There may be those who say that automakers will look for the best professionals in the market, with more experience and extensive knowledge. Considering the development of the financial market, it became impossible for professionals not to be finance experts. This only reinforces our argument that dependence on finance is a fundamental feature of the current economic age. Even in a company that manufactures cars, whose raw material is metal, plastic and glass, knowledge in the area of production becomes less important than knowledge in finance. Participation in banks and financial holding companies is more valued

Table 5.2 Origin of General Motors managers – 2015

Board of Directors	Organisations in which they participate or participated
Stephen J. Girsky Ex Vice President 2010 – 2014 Director since 2009	Centerbridge Partners, LP Morgan Stanley Dana Holdings Corporation
Linda R. Gooden Director since 2015	Lockheed Martin Corporation Automatic Data Processing, Inc. WGL Holdings, Inc.
Joseph Jimenez Jr Independent Director	Novartis AG Blackstone Group LP H. J. Heinz Company ConAgra Foods, Inc. The Clorox Company Colgate-Palmolive Company
Kathryn V. Marinello Director since 2009	Ares Management LLC Stream Global Services, Inc. Providence Equity Partners LLC Ceridian Corporation General Electric Company AB Volvo and Nielsen Holdings N.V. GE Capital Chemical Bank Citibank First Bank Systems, Inc.
James J. Mulva Director since 2012	ConocoPhillips General Electric Company Statoil ASA
Patricia F. Russo Director since 2009	Alcatel-Lucent S.A. Hewlett-Packard Company Alcoa, Inc. KKR Management LLC Merck & Co., Inc.
Carol M. Stephenson Director since 2009	Intact Financial Corporation Manitoba Telecom Services, Inc.
Thomas M. Schoewe Director since 2011	Wal-Mart Stores, Inc. Black & Decker Corporation KKR Management LLC Northrop Grumman Corporation PulteGroup, Inc

Source: General Motors Corporation, 2015b, pp.13 to 18.

than experience in mechanical, electrical engineering or deep, theoretical and tacit knowledge of how the automotive industry works.

Hyundai

Hyundai Motors is part of a family-type conglomerate, managed by four members of the same family and five external directors. Furthermore, differently from North American automakers, its main executives in 2016 did not pass through the world of finance but have always worked in a chaebol. President Mong Koo Chung was president of Kia and vice president of the Federation of South Korean industries. Her eldest son Eui Sun Chung is the vice president of Hyundai Motors, who was president of Kia Motors and studied for an MBA at the University of San Francisco, in the United States. Won Hee Lee was president of Hyundai Motors and has a master's degree in accounting from Western Illinois University in the United States. The passage through North American educational institutions is one of the strongest points of contact between this family group and financialised ideas.

Regarding the external directors, we can see in Table 5.3 that they are divided into legal, finance, strategy and marketing positions. They are prominent members of South Korean society, such as external legal director Se Bin Oh, who was once president of the country's supreme court. Besides him, there are representatives of professional associations and the regional tax office, trying to confer an external legitimacy to the automaker's business, since it has always had its governance considered to be of little trust, precisely because it is a family-type conglomerate that never had to be accountable to anyone, like the rest of the world. Noble (2010) says that the Board of Directors is restricted and dominated by members of the Chung family. For him "there is no movement towards the separation of ownership and management and Hyundai Motors and its closest subsidiaries remain a family affair". Quoting Stephen Ahn, an automotive analyst at Woori Investment & Securities, "Hyundai Motors depends on one man. Only he has the power to control management" (Noble, 2010, p.14).

Toyota

Contrary to what happens at Ford and GM, Toyota executives have no passages in the world of finance. Virtually all board members are mechanical engineers, physicists, economists, etc. (Table 5.4). CEO Akio Toyoda has a law degree and joined Toyota in 1984, while the other members joined even before him. Takeshi Uchiyamada, Chair of the board joined the company in 1969; Seiichi Sudo, Executive Vice President and

Table 5.3 Origin of Hyundai managers – 2016

Board of Directors	Organisations in which they participate or participated
Mong Koo Chung President and CEO	Honorary PhD from the National University of Mongolia in Business Management President and CEO of Kia Motors Corporation Vice President of the Korean Federation of Industries
Eui Sun Chung Vice president	MBA at the University of San Francisco President of Kia Motors
Won Hee Lee Permanent President	Master's in Accounting from Western Illinois University President of Hyundai Motor Company
Gap Han Yoon Permanent President	Graduated from Keimyung University President of the Hyundai Plant in Ulsan
Sung Il Nam External Strategy Director	PhD in Economics from the University of Rochester President of the Korean Association of Labour and Economics Professor of Economics at Sogang University
Se Bin Oh External Legal Director	Master's in Law Supreme Court Ex-President in Seoul Lawyer at Dongin Law Group
You Jae Yi External Marketing Director	MBA at Seoul National University President of the Korean Marketing Association Professor of Business Administration at Seoul University
Dong Kyu Lee External Legal Director	Adviser to Kim and Chang Law Group Secretary General of the Korean Fair Trade Commission
Byung Kook Lee External Finance Director	Seoul Regional Tax Office Commissioner President of e-Chon Tax Accounting Corp

Source: Hyundai Motor Company, 2016c.

Member of the Board of Directors, joined Toyota in 1974; Mitsuhisa Kato, Executive Vice President and Member of the Board of Directors, Chief officer, Frontier Research Centre, joined in 1975, and so on.

Almost all of them have made a career in the automotive sector and in industrial areas, which does not prevent them from practicing financialisation in several dimensions. The increasing participation of financial institutions and the payment of dividends to shareholders, which we will study below, show that financialisation is not carried out

Table 5.4 Origin of Toyota managers – 2016

Board of Directors	Organisations in which they participate or participated
Takeshi Uchiyamada Chairman of the Board of Directors	Graduated in Applied Physics at Nagoya University. He joined Toyota in April 1969. He is vice president of the Japanese Business Federation (Nippon Keidanren).
Akio Toyoda President, Member of the Board of Directors	Law degree from Keio University. MBA from Babson College, United States. He joined Toyota in 1984. He was vice president of NUMMI, a joint venture with GM in the United States.
Nobuyori Kodaira Executive Vice President, Member of the Board of Directors	Graduated in Economics from the University of Tokyo. Master's in Science from Cambridge University. He was a member of the Ministry of Foreign Trade and Industry (MITI) and director-general of the petroleum department. He joined Toyota as an advisor in 2008. Director of KDDI Corporation and member of the audit committee of Aichi Steel Corporation
Mitsuhisa Kato Executive Vice President, Member of the Board of Directors Chief officer, Frontier Research Centre	Graduated in Engineering from the University of Hokkaido. He joined Toyota in 1975. Chief engineer at Toyota's Vehicle Development Centre. Director of Toyota Boshoku Corporation, Hino Motors, Ltd., Daihatsu Motor Co, Ltd. and member of the audit committee of Aisin Seiki Co., Ltd.
Seiichi Sudo Executive Vice President, Member of the Board of Directors	Degree in Mechanical Engineering from the University of Tokyo. He joined Toyota in 1974.
Didier Leroy Executive Vice President, Member of the Board of Directors President, Business Unit Toyota No. 1 Chief Competitive Officer Chairman, Toyota Motor Europe NV/AS	Graduated in Engineering at the School of Science and Technology in Nancy, France. He joined Renault S.A. in 1982. He joined Toyota Motor Manufacturing France S.A.S in 1998.

Source: Toyota Motor Corporation, 2016b.

only by members who have passed through the world of finance, but can be practiced by anyone, provided that it becomes a natural and legitimately accepted issue by all the main actors involved in this process.

Volkswagen

Regarding the origin of VW's managers, there are also differences here compared to its leading competitors in the ranking of the world's largest automakers.

At Ford and GM, the main managers are members who started their careers at financial institutions and went to the automakers' Board of Directors afterwards, although there are also managers who have always been in the production area. At Hyundai and Toyota, managers come from factories and are engineers, economists, physicists and even lawyers, such as Toyota CEO Akio Toyoda.

At Volkswagen, there is a greater variety of professionals, but virtually all were or are members of the academy, professors with PhDs in their fields, which are engineering, computer science, business management and economics. However, the majority started their career already in the industrial area, as shown in the data in Table 5.5.

Table 5.5 Origin of Volkswagen managers – 2016

Board of Directors	Organisations in which they participate or participated
Matthias Müller Chairman of the Management Board of VW AG	Graduated in Computer Science at the University of Applied Sciences in Munich. Master's in Informatics. He joined Audi in 1978. He did practical training at the Ministry of Industry and Foreign Trade (MITI) in Japan in 1992. From 1993 he was head of project and product management at VW, Audi and Porsche.
Prof. Dr. rer. pol. Dr.-Ing. E. h. Jochem Heizmann Director of VW China	Graduated in Industrial Engineering from Karlsruhe University in 1975. University employee until 1982. Doctorate in Political Science in 1980. Joined Audi in 1982. Head of production planning and control at VW Passenger Cars in 1993. Member of the VW Management Board on projects in Russia and India. Developed new factories in the United States and China.

(*continued*)

Table 5.5 Cont.

Board of Directors	Organisations in which they participate or participated
Prof. Rupert Stadler Chairman of the Management Board of Audi AG	Graduated in Business Management, Controllership and Finance from the University of Applied Sciences in Augsburg. He joined Audi in 1990. Chairman of the Audi Management Board since 2007. Honorary Professor of Business Administration at the University of St. Gallen. Since 2010, member of the VW Management Board.
Dr. rer. pol. h.c. Francisco Javier Garcia Sanz Purchase Director	Graduated in Business Management at the Wiesbaden Business School. He joined Adam Opel in 1979 as a purchasing officer. Purchasing Director at GM. Chairman of the SEAT Board of Directors in 2007. Honorary doctorate from the University of Stuttgart.
Dr Karlheinz Blessing Member of the Management Board of Volkswagen AG with responsibility for the Human Resources and Organisation group – Joined January 2016	Graduated in Economics from the University of Konstanz. PhD in Economics and Social Sciences. He joined the management council of the German union IG Metall in 1984. He was general secretary of the German Social Democratic Party (SPD) from 1991 to 1993. He participated in several industry boards in the area of human resources and organisation.
Dr Robert Diess Member of the Management Board of VW AG since June 2015; Chairman of the Management Board for the VW Passenger Cars brand	Mechanical Engineer from the Technical University of Munich. He joined Bosch in 1989, BMW in 1996 and is a board member of BMW AG and VW Passenger Cars.

Source: Volkswagen AG, 2016.

Volkswagen has a big difference concerning the composition of managers. Concerning the participation of workers in the management, so popularised by corporate social responsibility, VW has as director of the human resources area, a former member of the national metallurgical union IG Metall, the largest German union, which represents almost 3 million workers and has great political strength in Germany. Executive Dr Karlheinz Blessing has a degree in economics and a doctorate in social sciences. He was a member of the IG Metall union and general secretary of the German Social Democratic Party (SPD).

This characteristic of the origin of the VW managers, having a workers' representative on its board, differs from all the other four automakers. At Ford, for example, on the contrary, there is a former governor of the Republican Party on the board, but there is nothing new about it, since he is a millionaire, and he was also a politician. There are no workers' representatives on the boards of the other four automakers, only when there is a pension fund involved and they participate through this fund. The case of VW seems to be different, presenting characteristics typical of German capitalism, which we have already highlighted in the chapter on shareholding composition, and which reflect a coordinated market economy, greater state intervention, with greater participation of workers in their decision-making centres and an apparent concern to make the representativeness of all stakeholders diverse.

6   Dividend payments to shareholders

The institution of joint-stock companies and the practice of investing in these shares as capital appreciation strategies have psychologically stimulated the expectation of a return to the shareholder as the main element. Investors have no interest in knowing the real situation of a company, its details, its history and that of its employees, bosses, suppliers or customers, in short, the individual, material and historical details that that enterprise acquired, but only the return that the company will give to its shares, its dividends and the appreciation of the stock over time.

The knowledge that investors in general hold about companies is summarised in their financial indicators and how they will be able to achieve their expectations of return, at which point the maximisation of shareholder value (Lazonick and O'Sullivan, 2000) becomes the main concern. Neoclassical economic theory states that the firm must pay dividends to shareholders, since all other stakeholders have been remunerated, in the form of salaries, interest, taxes, etc. The company would not pay dividends only if it did not make profits. It turns out that dividend payment decisions are not always linked, in practice, to the realisation of profits in that specific year. The company can have cash on hand and pay dividends in a year when there was no profit and at the same time decide to close factories, make layoffs, freeze wages, among other measures against workers, for example.

The company's executives and directors are partners of the shareholders as they define a set of remunerations and high compensation that are hundreds of times away from the mass wages of workers. In this case, what we see is an alliance between shareholders and directors of companies to enforce the principle of maximising shareholder value, ensuring that at the same time profits are distributed to shareholders through the payment of dividends and the bonuses and compensations to the managers are paid regularly.

DOI: 10.4324/9781003161141-6

In automobile manufacturers, despite the variety of origins of their directors, whether board members or just executives, the dividend payment policy has been strictly enforced, with a diligent concern to meet investors' expectations in the first place. Hence, financial metrics invaded the industrial environment with such force that they drained all their energies to achieve shareholder value creation. All the other concerns of the industrial age were left behind, in this new era marked by the maximisation of shareholder value.

Ford

Ford's shareholder remuneration policy was intensified in 2012. Since then, there has been a steady growth in earnings per share, which rose from US$0.20 in 2012 to US$0.40 in 2013, US$0.50 in 2014 and US$0.60 in 2015, thus tripling in four years (Table 6.1).

Such a return for a share that was worth around US$15.00 in 2016 and US$9 in 2020 may seem little, but when we see in Table 6.2 that the total net profit was distributed in the form of dividends to shareholders, we ask: how are the other business stakeholders?

These figures demonstrate that there is little left for reinvestments and salary improvements, among other advantages that could be distributed to its more than 187 thousand employees, such as the creation of a fund

Table 6.1 Dividends paid to shareholders – Ford

	2012	*2013*	*2014*	*2015*
EPS – earn per share in US$	0.20	0.40	0.50	0.60

Source: Nasdaq, 2016d.

Table 6.2 Net income and distribution to shareholders – Ford

	2012	*2013*	*2014*	*2015*	*2016*	*2017*	*2018*	*2019*
Net income in billions of US$	5,6	11,9	1,2	7,3	4,5	7,7	3,6	0,04
Value distributed to shareholders in billions of US$	5,6	11,9	1,2	7,3	4,5	7,7	3,6	0,04
% of net income distributed to shareholders	100	100	100	100	100	100	100	100

Source: Nasdaq, 2016e.

for times of crisis, through which cuts could be avoided, keeping jobs and avoiding thousands of layoffs. However, this hypothesis is ruled out by US automakers Ford and GM, as they have laid off thousands of workers in the past few decades, as we will see later in the chapter on workers' wages and the issue of employment.

General Motors

The policy of paying dividends to shareholders at General Motors, shortly after the US government bailout, developed in a similar way to that of Ford. As soon as the automaker started to make profits, after the 2008/2009 crisis, it immediately returned to valuing earnings per share. In 2010, as the reader can see in Table 6.3, the earn per share was US$2.89, almost doubling to US$4.58 in 2011, falling to US$2.92 in 2012, US$2.38 in 2013, US$1.65 in 2014 and rising to US$5.91 in 2015.

The distribution of net income also varied from year to year. However, in recent years the trend of distribution to shareholders has been increasing. It went from 78% of net profit in 2012 (when GM had US$6.1 billion in net profit and distributed US$4.8 billion to shareholders) to 70% in 2013 (with a net profit of US$5.3 billion and distribution of US$3.7 billion), 71% in 2014 (net profit of US$3.9 billion and distribution of US$2.8 billion) and 100% in 2015, when all net income of US$9.687 billion was distributed to shareholders. In 2016, all net income was distributed again; the only exception of the decade being in 2017, which presented a loss, due to the payment of income tax completely outside the automaker's standards, in the amount of US$11.5 billion. Were it not for this year, it would provide record profits for the company. Table 6.4 shows the figures for net income and the percentage that was distributed to shareholders.

It is worth mentioning that in 2018 and 2019, there was a distribution of net income in the form of dividend payments of 98% and 97%, respectively, confirming the growth trend in the MSV process.

Our work is not intended to make value judgments about what is right or wrong, because these concepts are relative and dependent on the views of each observer. Here we bring the numbers and try to break

Table 6.3 Dividends paid to shareholders – GM

	2010	*2011*	*2012*	*2013*	*2014*	*2015*
EPS – earn per share in US$	2.89	4.58	2.92	2.38	1.65	5.91

Source: Nasdaq, 2016f.

Table 6.4 Net income and distribution to shareholders – GM

	2012	2013	2014	2015	2016	2017	2018	2019
Net income in billions of US$	6,1	5,3	3,9	9,6	9,4	−3,8	8,0	6,7
Value distributed to shareholders in billions of US$	4,8	3,7	2,8	9,6	9,4	−3,8	7,9	6,5
% of net income distributed to shareholders	78	70	71	100	100	0	98	97

Source: Nasdaq, 2016g.

them down and analyse them using economic sociology tools, which aim to integrate the various social sciences for a better understanding of economic phenomena. What is certain is that depending on each dividend policy adopted by this or that company, their concrete reality will be x or y. Distributing the entire net profit to shareholders certainly has impacts that can be felt now or in the future. In the case of General Motors, we will see that this policy has already had significant impacts on the issue of employment, for example, since the company is very concerned with paying dividends, but not so much with maintaining the level of employment, with layoffs of more than 500,000 workers between 1988 and 2015, reducing a staff of approximately 800,000 employees to just over 200,000. If there were another dividend policy, with lower disbursements, certainly more jobs would be kept, maybe a fund to maintain jobs would be created to face moments of uncertainty and volatility in this consumption market. Would such intervention in the natural laws of markets be possible, or is it just a utopian dream with no practical consequences?

Hyundai

As part of the policy of gradual integration with financialisation, Hyundai is paying dividends to shareholders. Table 6.5 shows the number of dividends paid to shareholders compared to net income. So far, this amount is Hyundai's main difference from the other North American, Japanese and German automakers, as we will see below. The low rate of 6% of net income distributed to shareholders in 2012 and 2013 has been increasing significantly in recent years. In 2014, it went to 11% and then to almost 17% of net income in 2015. This is a clear commitment to the automaker's adaptation to the principles of maximising shareholder

Table 6.5 Net income and distribution to shareholders – Hyundai

	2012	2013	2014	2015
Net income in billions of US$	7,752	7,730	6,648	5,807
Value distributed to shareholders in billions of US$	0,471	0,483	0,739	0,976
% of net income distributed to shareholders	6.1	6.3	11.1	16.82

Source: Hyundai Motor Company, 2016d.

value. As already mentioned, the financialisation process at Hyundai seems to be late compared to the automakers Ford and GM, but also compared to Toyota and VW, as will be shown when we study these last two.

The company has been complying with corporate governance principles and this includes compliance with the dividend payments. As the company has a strong family dimension and millions of shares are held by the group's own family and companies, the pressures for an ever-greater return to shareholders have not been decisively felt until now. But with the change in the debt/stock ratio in favour of stocks recently, the need to respond to shareholders has been knocking on the door. At least 40% of common shares are said to be in the hands of foreign investors (Hyundai, 2016a, p.4). Hence the growth of more than 100% in the volume of dividends in just four years. Please note that even with falling net income, there was a significant increase in the distribution of dividends. In 2012, there was US$7.7 billion in net income and distribution of US$471 million in dividends. In 2015, with a net income of US$5.8 billion, that is, almost US$2 billion less, the volume of dividends was US$976 million, more than twice the amount distributed in 2012. Although in values significantly lower than competitors Ford and GM, the indication at Hyundai is for growth in the volume of dividend payments to shareholders.

Toyota

As stated in the paragraph above, even without a leading layer from the world of finance, Toyota's policy of maximising shareholder value has been rigorously practiced in recent years. Similar to Ford, Toyota distributed 100% of net profit to shareholders in the nine years between 2012 and 2020. There were almost US$140 billion in dividends paid. Little was left for reinvestments in substantial wage improvements or

Table 6.6 Net income and distribution to shareholders – Toyota

	2012	2013	2014	2015	2016	2017	2018	2019	2020
Net income in billions of US$	3,4	10,2	17,7	18,1	19,2	16,4	23,4	17	19,2
Value distributed to shareholders in billions of US$	3,4	10,2	17,7	18,1	19,2	16,4	23,4	17	19,2
% of net income distributed to shareholders	100	100	100	100	100	100	100	100	100

Source: Nasdaq, 2016h.

training. Table 6.6 shows the distribution of dividends to shareholders in recent years.

We can see from the data presented that the MSV is a major concern in the Japanese automaker, which has a very old link with financial organisations, dating back to the 1950s and 1960s. It turns out that in the case of Toyota, we saw that banks have an important role in the shareholding composition, and then come investment funds, notably passive funds. However, that did not change the fact that many more resources were allocated to shareholders and less in interest, for example.

Toyota has been paying an average of US$250 million a year in interest, US$5 billion in income tax and US$10 billion to US$20 billion annually in dividends (Nasdaq, 2020d), with these values by far the largest and which drain all net profit for shareholders, leaving all other stakeholders in the background.

Volkswagen

In this regard, Volkswagen is similar to Ford, GM and Toyota in that it has distributed almost all net income to shareholders in recent years. Table 6.7 shows the amount of net income and its distribution to shareholders.

As we can see, Volkswagen is the company that most distributed dividends to shareholders of all five automakers studied here in a short period. Approximately €57 billion (US$62 billion) was distributed in just four years. Even though it did not distribute 100% of net profit, similar to Ford, GM in most years and Toyota, Volkswagen's values were higher. It is a complete submission to the precepts of maximising shareholder value, which drains almost all the net profit, leaving the business

Table 6.7 Net income and distribution to shareholders – Volkswagen

	2011	2012	2013	2014
Net income in billions of Euros	15,799	21,884	9,145	11,068
Value distributed to shareholders in billions of Euros	15,409	21,717	9,066	10,847
% of net income distributed to shareholders	97.5	99.2	99.1	98

Source: Volkswagen AG, Annual Report, 2012, p.4; 2014, p.2.

unable to reinvest, better train its workforce, nor guarantee salary improvements and valorisation of the entire staff and collaborators.

If the prevailing thesis about Volkswagen was that there is an enormous resilience of productive operations considering the financialisation process, at least in this indicator, the German automaker behaved in the same way as North American and Japanese colleagues. Regarding dividend payments, Volkswagen's conduct is exemplarily aligned with the principle of MSV, as can be confirmed by all the data shown by us in this work.

7 Compensations to executives

This is a financialisation indicator considered to be very important because it refers to the power of decision within organisations. According to Bebchuk and Fried (2004), the payment of compensation to executives has little to do with the performance of the professional within the company, but with the power of decision. In the United States, the unification of the position of CEO with the presidency of the Board of Directors has reinforced this issue of power, since the main executive is also a member of the board and this directly influences the establishment of the values attributed to the executives (Webber, 2018). This privileged situation means that there is no limit to the compensation paid to executives, while on the basis of workers, salary stagnation seems to be the keynote of the relationship between capital and labour in recent years (International Labour Organisation, 2015).

Piketty (2014) had already described the process of creating a layer of leading millionaires at the top of the 0.1% of the income bracket and analysed that the speed of appreciation of these compensations to executives was greater than the appreciation of the wages of other workers, and this was an explanatory variable for the increase in economic inequality between incomes and across society. In automakers, this process is also present, as we will see in the five automakers.

Ford

At Ford, as in most of today's large companies, there is an annual salary for executives, long and short-term stock options, premiums entitled to restricted shares, in short, several millionaire compensations, making overall annual earnings of the managers compatible with the values received by the super-executives of the biggest companies, financial or not, but absurdly high in comparison with the remaining workers.

DOI: 10.4324/9781003161141-7

To have an idea of the compensation of the officers, we will take as an example six executives who had millionaire earnings in 2014. CEO Mark Fields received US$18.5 million only in the fiscal year of 2014, in salary and total compensation. Robert Shanks, executive vice president and chief financial officer, received US$6.3 million in total compensation. William Clay Ford Jr, the executive chairman, received US$15.1 million; James Farley Jr, executive vice president and division president for Europe, Middle East and Africa earned US$4.4 million in total compensation; Joseph Hinrichs, Ford's president for the Americas, pocketed US$6 million for the entire fiscal year of 2014, while Alan Mulally, former president and former CEO received US$22 million (Bloomberg, 2015).

It can be observed in Table 7.1 that the executives' cash wages were relatively low, compared to the total compensation they received. They ranged from US$800,000 to US$2 million. The largest amount, however, was paid in premiums through company shares, amounting to millions of dollars. This trend of fattening the executive compensation package with payments in shares has been observed in recent years. This leads to two results: 1) increase in the value of the shares, since a purchase movement affects the price of the shares positively and 2) collection of income tax only on the salary in cash, which is better for the executive and worse for the tax system.

General Motors

General Motors has the same executive compensation policy that several other large American companies apply and the same as Ford's. The automaker uses a comparison with the twenty largest companies, following four criteria. The first is to participate in the list of the 100 largest companies listed in Fortune magazine, with revenues ranging from US$30 billion to US$211 billion, with an average of US$59.9 billion in 2013. The second is to be a company "complex, with business operations that use a lot of capital intensive, including significant research and development, design, engineering and manufacturing functions with large numbers of employees". Third, to be a global company and fourth, to have broad participation in companies that manufacture products more than they provide services (General Motors, 2015b, p.44).

Among the 20 companies that have served as a benchmark for setting total compensation to managers are 3M, Boeing, Caterpillar, Ford, GE, HP, Pepsi, Johnson & Johnson, Pfizer and Procter & Gamble. See the compensations to executives in Table 7.2.

Table 7.1 Compensations to executives in US$ – Ford

Executive compensation In US$ 2014	Mark Fields CEO	Robert Shanks Executive Vice President CFO	William Clay Ford Jr Executive President	Joseph Hinrichs Vice President	James D. Farley Jr Vice President	Alan Mulally Former President Former CEO
Salary	1,662,500	798,750	2,000,000	936,250	868,750	1,000,000
Bonus	0.00	267,450	0.00	135,000	0.00	0.00
Share award	3,412,489	2,183,995	4,777,493	2,183,995	1,979,244	10,237,495
Stock options	6,249,994	799,995	1,749,996	799,995	724,994	3,749,994
Non-equity incentive plan	3,185,000	732,550	910,000	910,000	800,000	3,185,000
Change in pension value and profit not qualified deferred compensation	3,647,336	1,454,163	4,427,336	1,048,145	0.00	0.00
Other compensation	439,178	83,743	1,245,870	79,245	121,776	3,869,639
Total Compensations	18,596,497	6,320,646	15,110,695	6,092,630	4,494,764	22,042,128

Source: Ford Motor Company, 2015b, p.58.

Table 7.2 Compensations to executives in US$ – GM

	2014
Mary T. Barra Chief Executive Officer	16,162,828
Mark L. Reuss Global Executive Vice President and Product Development, Purchasing and Supply Chain	9,477,777
Daniel Ammann President and former Executive Vice President and Chief Financial Officer	8,489,346
Michael P. Millikin Executive Vice President and General Counsel	5,765,531

Karl-Thomas Neumann
Executive Vice President and President of the European
  division; Chairman of the Management Board of the
  Opel GmbH Group
	5,269,426

Charles K. Stevens, III Executive Vice President and Chief Financial Officer	4,894,832
Daniel F. Akerson Former President and CEO	2,099,253

Source: General Motors Corporation, 2015b, p. 52.

As with Ford, General Motors also has a fixed salary, plus short and long-term incentives and options, preferred shares and other bonuses that reach truly significant amounts. CEO Mary Barra received US$16.1 million in 2014. According to the company, these compensations are a set that privileges both personal and company performance. Issues such as market share, product quality, EBIT, are taken into account when determining earnings, according to official statements. Global executive vice president, Mark Reuss, received nearly US$9.5 million, almost the same amount from Daniel Ammann, former vice president and current chief financial officer, whose amounts reached US$8.4 million in total earnings.

We do not question here whether there is merit or not in setting these compensations. There may be those who say that they are fair because they are professionals of the highest standard. Besides, it would not be possible to measure exactly the amount that each employee adds to the business and how much they should receive. Therefore, the compensations, made up of a minimum fixed amount and the gross amount depending on performance, that is, a variable amount that is always at risk would be an adequate way of valuing the professional.

Democratic it is, because it is a decision endorsed by shareholders through their proxies, at annual meetings, say mainstream economists. The concrete fact is that it has become increasingly common for super executives to earn millions of dollars annually, whether in financial or manufacturing companies. What draws the most attention is that this exceptional appreciation depending on performance is not extended to all workers and other collaborators, but only to this select group of executives very well connected with the members of the Board, when they are not themselves the members the body that will set its compensation.

Hyundai

In this financialisation indicator, it seems that Hyundai is rapidly moving towards a pattern of compensation to its managers similar to the pattern of the North American market, which has been dictating the world average that occurs in the automotive sector. CEO Mong-Koo Chung received more than US$12 million in total compensation in 2014. It is the first time that his salary has been disclosed in years and years (Kim, 2014). The salaries of South Korean chaebols' tycoons had never been disclosed. With the increase in the participation of foreign shareholders, the demands for disclosure became higher. Even so, transparency is not complete. The vice president, his son Eui-Sun Chung, only had his earnings published by Hyundai Motors and Hyundai Mobis, but his earnings were not disclosed by Kia Motors, where he was president and holds a management position, nor Hyundai Steel, where he also holds a management position. Even so, their declared earnings exceeded US$2 million in 2014. The other senior directors did not have their earnings published either, but they probably represent levels similar to those of the president and vice president, since they are also permanent presidents, as shown in Table 7.3.

Although the CEO of Hyundai has received values comparable to those of Ford and GM executives, as we have seen before (US$18 million and US$16 million respectively), this is still not the standard of remuneration for other executives in the country, revealing yet another aspect of late financialisation that happens in South Korea. There, in the 500 largest companies, the average earnings of executives stood at US$600,000 annually, while in the USA the CEOs of the 500 largest companies earned an average of US$12 million in 2012 (Kim, 2014). It is a 20-fold difference that certainly tends to decrease as South Korean companies grow and adopt the practices of internationalised financial logic.

Table 7.3 Compensations to executives in US$ – Hyundai

Board of Directors	2014
Mong-Koo Chung President	4,907,975 – Hyundai Motors 3,680,981 – Hyundai Mobis 3,680,981 – Hyundai Steel 12,269,937 – Total compensation
Eui-Sun Chung Vice President	1,628,959.27 –Hyundai Motors 542,986.42 –Hyundai Mobis n/a – Hyundai Steel n/a – Kia Motors
Won Hee Lee Permanent President	n/d
Gap Han Yoon Permanent President	n/d

Source: Kim, 2014.

Toyota

In this regard, Toyota has been a little more moderate than its competitors. It is the automaker, of the five largest, that pays the least to its managers. While at Ford, GM and Hyundai, in addition to Volkswagen, which we will see next, the total earnings of the CEOs were between US$12 million and US$18 million in the fiscal year of 2014, at Toyota the CEO Akio Toyoda received in 2016 the value of US$3.4 million, a third of the value of his South Korean colleague at Hyundai, Mong-Koo Chung, who earned US$12.2 million in 2014.

At Toyota, there is also a peculiarity. The CEO has received less than one director, such as Didier Leroy, Executive Vice President, President of Toyota Business Unit No. 1, Chief competitive officer, Chairman of Toyota Motor Europe NV/AS. He graduated in Engineering from the School of Science and Technology in Nancy, France. He joined Renault S.A. in 1982. He joined Toyota Motor Manufacturing France S.A.S in 1998. In 2016, Didier Leroy received US$6.8 million, double the amount earned by CEO Akio Toyoda. Table 7.4 shows these values for 2016.

We make this reservation about the peculiarity only found in Toyota, which is that the CEO receives less than a vice-president director because in the other four automakers studied here this does not happen. The CEO always has the biggest payoffs of all. This is due, of course, to performance issues and differentiated criteria, which deserve further investigations in the future. For now, it is an interesting finding to make.

Table 7.4 Compensations to executives in US$ – Toyota

Board of Directors	2016
Akio Toyoda President, CEO	3,433,954.77
Didier Leroy Executive Vice President	6,828,664.35
Mitsuhisa Kato Executive Vice President	1,412,827.11
Seiichi Sudo Executive Vice President	1,226,412.42
Shigeki Terashi Executive Vice President	1,147,922.02
Takahiro Ijichi Executive Vice President	981,129.93

Source: Morningstar, 2016. Cuex, 2016. US$ 1 = JPY 101,85.

Volkswagen

Compensation to Volkswagen executives follows the level of North Americans, Ford and GM, followed by Hyundai, which for the first time in history released the earnings of CEO Mong-Koo Chung, whose earnings were more than US$12 million in 2014, as seen previously.

The then CEO Martin Winterkorn received more than €15 million in the fiscal year 2014, around US$19.5 million, higher than that earned by Mary Barra, from GM (US$16 million) and Mark Fields, from Ford (US$18 million). These compensations are related to the average of companies in the automotive sector, with the exception of Toyota, which, as we have seen, pays three to four times less to its managers than the average of the automakers.

Table 7.5 shows the compensation received by Volkswagen executives in 2014.

As can be seen in Table 7.5, the compensation is also millionaire at Volkswagen, ranging from 4 to 15 million euros (5 to 19 million dollars) for the main members of the board. These compensations refer to fixed and variable gains and change according to performance, in the same way as in other automakers. In the case of Volkswagen, after the 2015 crisis, with the diesel scandal, there was a loss for the company and, therefore, for shareholders, of more than €1.5 billion and that figure has increased to this day. Compensations also fell, with CEO Matthias

Table 7.5 Compensations to executives in US$ – Volkswagen

Board of Directors	2014
Martin Winterkorn Chairman of the Management, Research and Development Council	19,509,617.94
Leif Östling Commercial Vehicle Director	9,453,912.84
Francisco Javier Garcia Sanz Procurement Director	9,064,081.56
Christian Klingler Sales and Marketing Director	8,987,157.36
Jochen Heizmann VW China Director	8,896,588.77
Rupert Stadler Chairman of the Management Board of Audi AG	8,486,196.81
Hans Dieter Pötsch Finance and Control Director	8,363,837.64
Horst Neumann Human Resources and Organisation Director	7,973,160.12
Michael Macht Production Director	5,323,480.59

Source: Volkswagen AG, Annual Report, 2014, pp.61–63. 1 euro = 1.23 dollar on 17 December 2014.

Müller receiving at the end of the fiscal year of 2016 around €4.7 million, well below its predecessor two years earlier (Volkswagen, 2015, p.69).

What we can deduce from all these data on executive compensation is that not all literature is right when it says that payment and performance are unrelated, but only the power to decide is what counts. In the same way that the financial sector acquires relative and not absolute autonomy over the "real" economy since they are very interconnected (Mollo, 2011), the compensations are in a way also anchored on a real basis linked to performance. Because if it were the other way around, we would see that in years of losses, (when such stratospheric compensation was not paid) the compensation would also tend to be exaggerated. This has not happened, which leads us to believe that shareholders, even carrying out a policy of enriching a layer of super executives, are susceptible to market fluctuations and moods. It is not good to pay millions of dollars of compensation in years of loss, hence their restraint at these times.

This does not mean that the power to decide is not important, as Bebchuk and Fried (2004) have defined well. It is through the power to decide between board members and top executives that compensation has been set in the millions of dollars annually. This trend has been very strong, and we have witnessed this process with the concern that it will increase economic and social inequality.

8   Employees' salaries and employment

One concern of this book is how the fruits and results of business activities are distributed. For example, how companies distribute their profits, pay salaries, dividends and compensation to executives. That is, we want to see how stakeholders have their compensation paid. We have already addressed dividend payments to shareholders, compensation paid to executives and now we will turn to salaries paid to workers, and their subsequent comparison with the total earnings of CEOs. Therefore, the level of the salary difference between the main executive and the rest of the employees will be observed.

The level of employment is also a concern since it is one of the indicators that the financial pole is more important than the productive pole, given that it is one of the first victims at a time of cutting costs or saving resources. Although the level of employment alone is not defined by the financialisation process as many automobile manufacturers worldwide have hired workers in the last decades, while others have laid many off in the same period. The fact is that in this indicator there are multiple dynamics of financialisation, with each company presenting different conducts and this only makes the process richer and more interesting to analyse. We will see the data presented on workers' wages, their comparison with the CEOs' total earnings and then the data on employment.

Ford

In 2015, Ford had around 187 thousand employees and most of them belonged to the production level. Moreover, the factory floor had more than 60% of the total employees. The employees in this category, who were the majority, had starting salaries that we can consider low for an industrial category that has always been highly valued in terms of salaries. In that year, grassroots employees received around US$17,000

DOI: 10.4324/9781003161141-8

Table 8.1 Employee salaries – Ford

Professional	Annual in US$ – August 2015 to December 2020	
	Minimum	Maximum
Service Assistant	17,881	57,320
Administrative Assistant	24,834	46,801
Assembler	25,907	68,086
Electrical Engineer	66,000	122,000
Supervisor Engineer	64,535	154,628
Group Manager of Engineers	90,301	190,429

Source: Payscale, 2015.

annually for a novice service assistant, including the assembly line worker, who earned an initial US$25,000 annually. An electrical engineer earned an initial US$67,000 annually, a supervising engineer earned US$64,000 annually, until he/she reached a group manager of engineers, with starting salaries of US$90,000, as shown in Table 8.1 (Payscale, 2015).

Based on the salary data released by the Payscale website, we can see the minimum and maximum amounts paid by Ford that were presented. These numbers change throughout the year and we based them on August 2015. In a quick and new survey on the same topic carried out in 2020, we see that little has changed in Ford's salary policy, as a mechanical engineer received an initial salary of US$66,000 annually; a product development engineer earned an initial salary of US$69,000 and a software engineer received an initial salary of US$63,000 annually. Recall that the average salary of all North American ethnic groups in 2019 was US$68,000 (Statista, 2020). That is, a Ford engineer received starting salaries less than or equal to the average salary for all ethnic groups, a situation of stagnation compared to previous decades, as in 1947 a General Motors worker received 20% more than the average of all salaries and today earns 60% of that average (Wartzman, 2017).

It can be observed that there is a wage gap between workers, which is normal in a capitalist economic system, where there are even differences between the distribution of resources between individuals and their professions. At Ford, the wage gap between a less qualified worker and a more qualified worker is around four to five times, as can be seen in Table 8.1.

When we compare employee salaries with the total compensation that executives receive, especially the chief executive officer (CEO), we

Table 8.2 Ratio of times between employee salaries and total earnings for a CEO – Mark Fields, Ford – US$18,596,497 – 2014

Professional	2014		
	Minimum	Maximum	Average
Service Assistant	324	1040	682
Administrative Assistant	397	748	572
Assembler	273	717	495
Electrical Engineer	126	273	199
Supervisor Engineer	120	288	204
Group Manager of Engineers	97	205	151

Source: authors, based on the comparison of the data in the tables "Total compensation to directors and executives (annual)" and "Employee salaries – annual in US$".

see a huge disparity, reaching 1040 times the salary difference between the CEO and the simplest worker, as shown in Table 8.2.

Table 8.2 shows the ratio of times between employees' salaries and the total earnings of the CEO and indicates the minimum and maximum times ratio since our salary source distinguishes between the minimum and maximum wages in the company, according to the position, function and working time. Hence, we prefer to establish a general average to find a midpoint of the wage gap between managers and other employees. The fact that a CEO earns an average of 682 times more than a service assistant is noteworthy; 572 times more than an administrative assistant; 495 times more than an assembler; 199 times more than an electrical engineer; 204 times more than a supervising engineer and 151 times more than a group manager of engineers.

These salary differences are expected to have considerable impacts on the company's internal governance and power relations. Or, on the contrary, they may be a direct effect of the financialised governance model and power relations. This seems to be one of the characteristics of financialisation. Concerning the workforce used in the business, in the case of Ford, financialisation was classic, in the sense of disposing of fixed assets and also of the workforce, reducing the tangible resources to increase financial assets, at the expense of thousands of jobs. Figure 8.1 shows the employment data at Ford from 2000, where we see a significant drop in the number of employees.

As the data in Figure 8.1 shows, in 2001 Ford employed 358,000 workers and had this number reduced year after year throughout the 2000s. In 2010, it reached its lowest number, which was 164,000 workers. A 54.19% drop in jobs, that is, almost 200,000 workers were laid off in

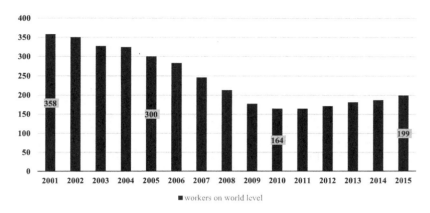

Figure 8.1 Evolution of employment at Ford – in thousands
Source: Ford Annual Reports, 2002–2015.

just a decade. In the current decade, there has been a small increase in the number of jobs at the automaker. In 2015, the company employed 199,000 workers worldwide. This is a scenario that we call classic because even in moments of production growth, the company cut vacancies. This can be credited to the company's productivity increase, but it can also be the result of conscious decisions taken to reduce even the productive pole in favour of an appreciation and returns to shareholders through financial activities, as we saw in the first chapter of this book.

General Motors

General Motors employees' salaries closely resemble those of Ford, as seen earlier. The lowest salaries in 2016 were those of service technicians, which ranged between US$18,000 and US$42,000 annually, including assemblers, who earned between US$22,000 and US$52,000, in addition to administrative assistants, who received between US$23,000 and US$52,000 a year. This gave an average of US$30,000 for technicians, US$37,000 for assemblers and US$39,000 for assistants yearly. They were well below the overall average American wages for all ethnic groups, which in 2016 was US$57,000 (Guzman, 2017) and in 2019 was US$68,000 (Statista, 2020).

As shown in Table 8.3, only when we consider engineer positions does the value increase. In the case of an electrical engineer, earnings ranged between US$59,000 and US$102,000, an average of US$80,500

Table 8.3 Employee salaries – GM

Professional	Annual in US$ – March 2016 to December 2020	
	Minimum	Maximum
Automotive Service Technician	18,252	42,386
Assembler	22,797	52,045
Administrative Assistant	23,882	52,350
Electrical Engineer	59,036	102,124
Mechanical Engineer	67,759	125,831
Group Manager of Engineers	109,352	196,172

Source: Payscale, 2020.

annually. A mechanical engineer was paid US$67,000 to US$125,000, with an annual average of US$96,000. Moreover, an engineer group manager's salary ranged from US$109,000 to US$196,000, an annual average of US$152,500. These were three times above the national average salary, which in 2016 was US$57,000, as previously seen. In 2020, some maximum values even fell in some positions, such as that of a mechanical engineer, which went up to US$125,000 in 2016 and has now gone up to US$103,000.

Again, we are not here to attribute value judgment, but only to analyse the actual occurrence of wage composition at General Motors. When we advanced our research and endeavoured to compare the automaker's overall salaries with the managers' earnings and compensation, just as in the case of Ford, there was a significant difference. Table 8.4 estimates the proportion of times the CEO earns compared to the salaries of the remaining employees. In this table, we list some functions that are essential to the company's progress. Furthermore, the differences also reach hundreds of times.

The average number of times the CEO earns compared to other employees is also huge at GM, as well as at Ford. Between a top manager and a service technician, there was a difference of 633 times in 2014. Concerning an assembler, a CEO earned an average of 509 times more. An administrative assistant received 492 times less than a CEO, who earned 215 times more than an electrical engineer, 183 times more than a mechanical engineer and 114 times more on average than an engineer group manager.

This debate is old and leads us to the composition of remunerations. According to the Marxist tradition, salaries are a commodity like any other and, as such, their value is fixed by the labour time socially

Table 8.4 Ratio of times between employee salaries and total CEO earnings –
Mary Barra, GM – US$16,162,828 – 2014

Professional	2014		
	Minimum	Maximum	Average
Automotive Service Technician	381	885	633
Assembler	310	708	509
Administrative Assistant	308	676	492
Electrical Engineer	158	273	215
Mechanical Engineer	128	238	183
Group Manager of Engineers	82	147	114

Source: authors, based on the comparison of the data in the tables "Total compensation
to directors and executives (annual)" and "Employee salaries – annual in US$".

necessary for the production. In the case of wages, "manufacturing" is
the set of expenses necessary to train that workforce. If a worker earns
an average of US$30,000 to US$40,000 annually, it is because his/her
cost of production was approximately that. The same goes for engineers,
whose training takes longer and is more expensive, hence their remuneration is higher. For the neoclassical tradition, the labour commodity is
not related to the cost of production, but the supply and demand of
professionals in the market. If there are more assembly workers than the
number of vacancies offered, the salary will fall, even below the socially
necessary time spent on its production. If there are few workers with
this qualification in the market, the tendency is for their remuneration
to be higher.

And what determines the price formation of the executive's labour?
Is his or her background much better than that of a group manager of
engineers? Sometimes it is, but in general, these super-executives have
training similar to that of economists, engineers and other professionals
whose cost of training is similar. Therefore, why do they earn hundreds
of times more? Certainly, the answer has to do with what we discussed
above, in terms of the supply and demand of these professionals in the
market. Add to that the risks, and personal and company performance
they take, as well as the experience in financial groups and gigantic
corporations. And, of course, the old and good influence in defining
their peers' earnings. But even so, this question remains open for future
debates and its reality is not something natural and immutable, but
socially constructed so that what is in force tomorrow may not be.

Last but not least, the issue of employment emerges with resounding
clarity. If, for many analysts, the issue of employment is determined

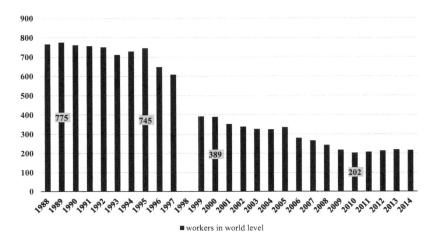

Figure 8.2 Evolution of employment at General Motors – in thousands
Source: General Motors Corporation, Annual Reports, 2003–2014; data for 1988–2002 from Froud et al., 2006, p.289, table C.2.5.

by variations in demand and the consumer market, what matters is to always produce with lower payroll expenses. That is what GM has been doing for the past 30 years. For the company, layoffs, factory closures and restructuring were not a problem, as it remained firm and strong, almost going bankrupt in 2009, but regaining its vigour, even if it was necessary to cut overtime of no less than two-thirds of its workforce. Figure 8.2 shows the evolution, or rather, involution, of employment at General Motors over almost three decades.

GM employed 775,000 workers in 1989, dropping to 608,000 in 1997 and falling to 352,000 in 2001. After that, it fell even more, dropping to an average of 200,000 workers worldwide in 2010. This demonstrates well that it is a drastic cut of a giant and traditional automotive company in its employment levels. GM accompanied Ford in reducing its workforce, albeit in huge doses, as more than two-thirds of its workforce has been evaporated from the company. The traditional explanation is that labour productivity always explains job cuts, however what happened was an escape from the United States and other rich countries to poor and developing countries, such as Eastern Europe, Mexico, Brazil, among others, that showed General Motors was hiring, but with salaries well below those paid in rich countries. It is obvious that the search for productivity and cost cuts has always existed, and has been occurring, but increasingly at the expense of lowering the quality of work and life of large masses of workers.

Hyundai

To analyse the salaries of Hyundai employees in South Korea, the headquarters of the automaker, we will use three factory professionals in Korea, four professionals at the United States plant, in the state of Alabama and two at the Indian plant in Tamil Nadu. The latter accounted for 12.3% of Hyundai's total production in 2014, reaching 611,000 units produced, second only to South Korea (1,876,000 units produced, 37.9% of the total) and from China, which accounted for 22.6% of Hyundai's world production, or 1,120,000 units produced in 2014 (Hyundai, 2014, p.5).

Table 8.5 shows the minimum and maximum values found in some professions in the South Korean automaker. In India, wages are shown on average.

We use the salary of an assembler in Alabama, United States, as there is a lack of data for the assembler in the host country. However, judging by an engineer's salary we found in Korea, which is lower than that of an assembler in the United States (both from Hyundai), it appears that the salaries of Hyundai assemblers in South Korea are lower than the salaries of Hyundai assemblers in other countries, such as the United States and India. Salaries in North American and Indian Hyundai are much higher than salaries at Ford and GM for the same positions.

Table 8.5 Employee salaries – Hyundai

Professional	Annual in US$ – 2016	
	Minimum	*Maximum*
R&D Engineer – South Korea	30,700	63,300
Management Assistant – South Korea	49,400	53,100
Senior Research Manager – South Korea	58,800	82,200
Assembler – Alabama, USA	52,000	56,000
Process Engineer – Alabama, USA	57,000	63,000
Hired hourly – Alabama, USA	9.00	10.00
Process Control Specialist – Alabama, USA	52,000	57,000
Mechanical Engineer – India	Average	96,000
Sales Manager – India	Average	218,000
Quality Engineer – China	140,278.32	149,270

Sources: Careerbliss, 2016; Glassdoor, 2016a,b.

The average US$54,000 annual value of an assembler in Alabama is equivalent to US$26 an hour, which is 57% above the average of all assembly line wages in the United States and 12% below the average of all American workers' wages in the United States (Careerbliss, 2016). That is, the salary of an assembler in the United States is higher than that of a Hyundai engineer in Korea.

In 2014, the average annual salary in South Korea was US$36,492, already adjusted by the purchasing power parity (Yoon, 2020). In 2019, that amount rose to US$42,285 annually. If we take the amount paid to workers in Korea, we will see that an initial R&D engineer in South Korea received US$30,000 in 2014, when the country's average salary was US$36,000. That is, the wage figures for Hyundai workers in South Korea were below the average annual value for all wages in the country.

This fact goes back to the previous discussion about what constitutes the price of salary merchandise. We can see that, in the case of Hyundai, the mainstream thesis of supply and demand in the labour market must be the most applicable because in South Korea there must be a huge supply of engineers and other qualified professionals willing to work for an initial amount of US$30,000 a year. Perhaps in India, this professional is not so easily found as a mechanical engineer at Hyundai in India earns an average of US$96,000. These data open up possibilities for further research on workers' wages in a very important sector such as the automotive sector.

The fact is that, with base wages better than Ford and GM, at least in countries where Hyundai has factories, the inequality between workers' wages and the total earnings of a CEO was not as great as in the United States, but yet they reached hundreds of times.

Table 8.6 shows the difference in times between the earnings of Hyundai's CEO and other workers.

The differences between earnings are huge when we see that the CEO earned at least 527 times on average more than an hourly worker, the least valued, who received US$9 to US$10 an hour in 2014. The difference between one and the other reaches 230 times the CEO's gain compared to an Alabama assembler; 210 times more than a process engineer, and 230 times more compared to the process control specialist. On average, the CEO received 125 times more than a mechanical engineer in India and 55 times more than an Indian sales manager. It is a wage situation that is very similar to that of North American automakers, although with a greater appreciation. This can be considered more of a late financialisation factor that affects Hyundai less than its North American competitors. However, the glaring differences between the

Table 8.6 Ratio of times between employee salaries and total CEO earnings –
Mong-Koo Chung, Hyundai – US$12,269,937 – 2014

Professional	2014		
	Minimum	Maximum	Average
R&D Engineer – South Korea	390	189	289
Management Assistant – South Korea	242	225	233
Senior Research Manager – South Korea	204	145	174
Assembler – Alabama, USA	230	214	222
Process Engineer – Alabama, USA	210	190	200
Hired hourly – Alabama, USA	555	500	527
Process Control Specialist – Alabama, USA	230	210	220
Mechanical Engineer – India	n/d	n/d	125
Sales Manager – India	n/d	n/d	55
Quality Engineer – China	85	80	83

Source: authors, based on the comparison of the data in the tables "Total compensation
to directors and executives (annual)" and "Employee salaries – annual in US$".

CEO's earnings and the earnings of various positions remain a common
characteristic for all automakers worldwide.

In the case of the employment level at Hyundai, the trend is for
growth, compared to its North American competitors. In recent years,
the South Korean automaker increased its workforce from 75,000
workers in 2011 to 104,000 in 2013, 109,000 in 2014 and 112,000 in
2015. In 2016, the number rose to 118,000 and in 2017 it was 129,000
workers. From this total, around 40% is abroad, in countries such as the
United States, China, India, Russia, Brazil, that is, the bulk of the world
market, which has allowed the automaker to meet its aim of being an
automobile company among the largest in the world.

Toyota

Table 8.7 shows six types of jobs and salaries at Toyota factories in Japan
and the United States. In the same way as Hyundai, for example, Toyota
also pays differently, depending on the country in which its plants are
located and the wage level in force in each country. A Toyota engineer
in the United States earns an average of US$82,500, while in Japan,
the same engineer earns an average of US$58,000. In general, salaries
are lower in Japan than abroad, even to accompany Ford and GM salaries, in the case of engineers, managers and supervisors. In the case
of an assembler's wages, one of the most numerous within the factory,

Table 8.7 Employee salaries – Toyota

Professional	2016 to 2020	
	Minimum	Maximum
Engineer – USA	55,000	110,000
Specialist – USA	54,000	89,000
US hourly production team member	15.00	30.00
Assembler – Texas, USA	24,000	35,000
Assistant Manager – Japan	56,700	61,500
Engineer – Japan	56,120	61,500
Assembler – Japan (2020)	16,900	101,000

Sources: Glassdoor, 2016c,e; Salary Explorer, 2020.

Toyota pays, in the United States, an average of US$29,500 per year, less than Ford (annual average of US$47,000) and GM (annual average of US$37,000), as we saw before (Glassdoor, 2016c,e).

In Japan, the wage struggle is reduced because the country has already been through a deflationary process for some years. This causes difficulties for salary increases, which would be against economic reality. To have an idea of the Japanese wage issue at Toyota, let us remember the case of 2014, in which the company considered having granted the biggest increase in the last 21 years to workers, whose claim was 4,000 yen (US$40.00) per month to more, but only managed 2,700 yen (US$27.00) a month. In other words, an entire struggle to achieve an average 0.8% increase for all workers (Reuters, 2014).

Koichi Shimizu, a professor at Okayama University, says that there has been a profound change in the salary system at Toyota since 2004 and that the new policy could represent the end of Ohnoism, referring to Taiichi Ohno, founder of the Toyota Production System and who established an individual valuation system, a major Toyota differential, which is gradually being dismantled (Shimizu, 2015).

Average wages in Japan were US$37,800 a year in 2019 (Kawano, 2019). We will see that an assembly line worker's salary in Japan, in general, starts at US$16,000 per year, but has an average of US$40,000 (Salary Explorer, 2020) and a maximum of US$101,000, which is a good average and a maximum salary. However, the initial salary is well below the national average salary of US$37,800. Table 8.7 shows these numbers.

The rest of Toyota's starting salaries in Japan for engineers and managers is above Japanese average salaries in 2019, as we have just seen. This shows that at least in the intermediate categories there is a good salary increase.

Table 8.8 Ratio of times between employee salaries and total CEO earnings – Akio Toyoda, Toyota – US$2,840,000 – 2014

Professional	2016 to 2020		
	Minimum	Maximum	Average
Engineer – USA	62	31	46
Specialist – USA	63	38	50
US hourly production team member	95	47	76
Assembler – Texas, USA	143	98	120
Assistant Manager – Japan	60	55	57
Engineer – Japan	61	55	58
Assembler – Japan (2020)	168	28	120

Source: authors, based on the comparison of the data in the tables "Total compensation to directors and executives (annual)" and "Employee salaries - annual in US$".

Table 8.8 shows the proportion of times more that a CEO earns in relation to the employees listed in the previous table. At Toyota, there is also a significant difference between the number of times between the CEOs earnings and all other positions. However, as the CEO's earnings are not so high, compared to the other CEOs of the other automakers studied here, the number of times from the highest to the lowest salary is much less than in the other four manufacturers. At Toyota, we found a minimum difference of 31 times and a maximum of 143 times the earnings of the CEO compared to other salaries.

There is a huge wage gap between the CEO and the assembler of Toyota at the plant in Texas, United States. It reaches 143 times the wage gap. The shortest gap between earnings is between the CEO and the engineer at the plant in the United States. This is 31 times the total compensation of CEO Akio Toyoda compared to the annual salary of an engineer in the United States.

Only by analysing these figures can we minimally conclude that the wage gap at Toyota is much smaller than at the other automakers studied here, including at Hyundai, as the remuneration of the CEO at Toyota is three to four times less than that of its competitors. Nor does it compare with Ford and GM, who showed wage differences of the order of 700 to 1000 times between the CEO and the least paid worker.

Concerning the level of employment at Toyota, unlike North American automakers, which dropped their number of employees over the past two decades, the Japanese automaker has increased its number of workers by at least 25% in ten years (Figure 8.3).

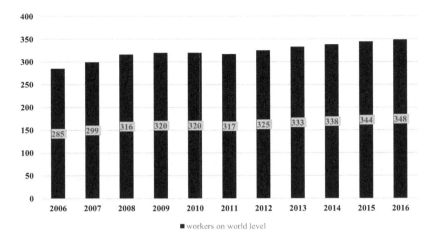

Figure 8.3 Evolution of employment at Toyota – in thousands
Source: Toyota Annual Report, several years.

Toyota employed 285,000 workers in 2006, this number increased to 320,000 in 2010, and then dropped to 317,000 in 2011. The number of workers has been growing year after year, reaching 348,877 workers worldwide in 2016. This is a company that has maintained its dependence on mass workers to be able to meet the demand, and thus manage to beat the competition, which today is between it and Volkswagen in the struggle for leadership. Here, in this financialisation indicator, we cannot say that this process has destroyed jobs, as we also saw at Hyundai, which has been hiring year after year. In addition, we will see that the next company to be analysed, Volkswagen, was the company that hired the most in recent years, leaving only the North American Ford and GM as "job destroyers", among the five largest automakers at the worldwide level.

Volkswagen

In the same way, as in other automakers, Volkswagen pays different salaries for the same functions in different countries where it operates. Table 8.9 shows these values.

As can be seen, Volkswagen's wages for less-skilled workers are lower or, at least, equal to those of other automakers. A common production worker receives between 24,000 and 36,000 euros per year. At

Table 8.9 Employee salaries – Volkswagen

Professional	Annual in euro -2016	
	Minimum	Maximum
Manager – Germany	61,000	100,000
Project Manager – Germany	84,000	116,000
Production Worker – Germany	24,000	36,000
Purchasing Officer – China	19,313	22,532
Senior Purchasing Officer – China	30,982	33,664
Engineer – Brazil	22,978	26,261
Software Engineer – Los Angeles, USA	63,534	68,903

Sources: Glassdoor, 2016d, Payscale, 2016.

Table 8.10 Ratio of times between employee salaries and total CEO earnings – Martin Winterkorn, Volkswagen – US$19.5 million/18 million euros

Professional	2014		
	Minimum	Maximum	Average
Manager – Germany	260	158	209
Project Manager – Germany	188	136	162
Production Worker – Germany	660	440	550
Purchasing Officer – China	821	703	762
Senior Purchasing Officer – China	511	471	491
Engineer – Brazil	690	603	646
Software Engineer – Los Angeles – USA	249	230	240

Source: authors, based on the comparison of the data in the tables "Total compensation to directors and executives (annual)" and "Employee salaries – annual in US$".

Volkswagen's factories in China, the figures are even lower. A purchasing officer earns 19,000 euros a year. When comparing engineers' wages, we see that there are huge differences between the factories located in different countries. An engineer in Brazil earns between 22,000 and 26,000 euros per year. A software engineer in the United States, on the other hand, earns between 63,000 and 68,000 euros a year.

In spite of the wage differences between Volkswagen factories in different countries around the world, the fact is that, when compared to the total earnings of the CEO, for example, there is a huge difference between the earnings of the top manager and the wages of the least qualified workers. In Table 8.10 we see the number of times more the CEO earns compared to other positions of the automaker.

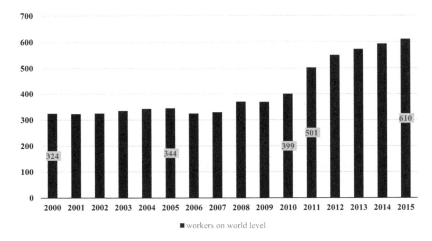

Figure 8.4 Evolution of employment at Volkswagen – in thousands
Source: VW Annual Reports, several years.

The minor differences amount to 136 times the CEO's earnings compared to a project manager in Germany, for example. Moreover, the earnings can reach 821 times those of the CEO when compared to a purchasing officer in China. In Brazil, an engineer earns 690 times less than a CEO in 2014. These differences fall when compared to the salaries of a software engineer in the United States, reaching 230 times his/her salaries compared to the earnings of the CEO. Finally, Volkswagen repeats the degree of inequality presented by the other automakers, except for Toyota, which is much less unequal because of the much lower compensation from the CEO.

When we analyse Volkswagen's employment levels, we see that the German automaker is by far the one that most expanded its job base both in Germany and in the rest of the world. Figure 8.4 shows the growth in the number of workers at Volkswagen.

The German automaker had 324 thousand workers in 2000, reaching 399 thousand in 2010, around a 23% growth in a decade. In 2011, it jumped to 501 thousand; in 2012 to 549 thousand; in 2013 to 572 thousand; in 2014 to 592 thousand and in 2015 it employed 610 thousand workers worldwide. This jump in the decade of 2010 has to do with its Joint Ventures in China and represents an increase of 88% in the number of workers from 2000 to 2015. In 15 years, Volkswagen made, for example, the opposite movement to that carried out by rival General Motors and, to a lesser extent, Ford.

These figures on employment at automakers reflect a process full of specificities and allow for multiple dynamics in this indicator, where each company behaves differently, as two automakers cut jobs (Ford and GM), while two increased their employment levels relatively well (Hyundai and Toyota) and another significantly increased its jobs, in Germany and abroad (Volkswagen). These results demonstrate that the financialisation process in the automotive sector is more complex than we might have assumed at the beginning of our research.

9 Conclusions

Ford

The first conclusion from our study on Ford's financialisation is that it is a growing process and has been intensifying each year. The dependence of the financial sector is visible as we demonstrate in the analysis category that compared the sources of profitability. Ford Financial is the sector that proportionally gives the automaker more profits and this has been happening, with ups and downs, for at least 25 years, as can be seen from the company's annual reports and studies by Froud et al. (2006).

Ford's shareholding composition shows that few and large financial groups, which operate in various sectors of the world economy, increasingly expand their participation in the automaker's property rights. Just over 1% of large investors have more than half of the shares and great decision-making power, concentrating huge economic resources, thus defining their investment and business strategies, as well as destinations of the car manufacturer.

The acquisitions also prove that more and more financial-type organisations are advancing in shareholding and expanding their actions. The biggest acquisitions in recent years were made by large banks and passive investment funds, among others, and reflect the movements that the financial sector has been making in the rights of the automaker Ford, which starts to depend more and more on the world of finance, subordinating the production to the interests of the controllers, that is, an ever-greater return on shareholders' investments.

The company's directors largely come from the world of finance and bring their financialised mentality to the company, facilitating the way to maximise shareholder return, which has become a true ideology, absorbing 100% of the automaker's net profit in the year from 2012 to 2015. Fligstein (1991) debates this issue in his work on the transformations of the North American industry.

DOI: 10.4324/9781003161141-9

Compensations to company directors are in the order of millions of dollars each year, and when compared to the salaries of other workers, they reveal a salary gap that can reach more than a thousand times the difference between the CEO's earnings, for example and a worker with less skills and qualifications.

The dividend payment policy to shareholders reflects this exclusive concern with the return to shareholders at the expense of any other factors involved in the business and is what was called the new ideology of the corporate world by Lazonick and O'Sullivan (2000). Since 2012, Ford has been distributing 100% of its net profit to shareholders. Very little remains for reinvestments and wage improvements. Such a mentality creates a climate of instability and lack of security about tomorrow, as now the company can make profits, and then share them under the aegis of maximising shareholder return. Sometimes it can cause losses, compromising jobs, equity, wages and other assets, as we saw in the case of the level of employment, which declined by more than 50% in just 15 years.

General Motors

After decomposing all five categories that make up the financialisation process, listed above, we can conclude that at General Motors this process is as powerful as at Ford. The comparison between the revenues of the productive sector and the financial sector enables us to recognise that the profits from financial activities are higher, in terms of percentage, than the profits from productive activities. In some years it was ten times higher, reaching a 45% return on financial income. Even so, the accumulated value of those who invested US$100 in 2010 would be nil, regressing to US$99 in December 2015. Meanwhile, the Dow Jones and S&P 500 indices yielded 31% and 80.5% respectively, in five years. The analyses by Froud et al. (2006) were correct, in the sense that the profitability of the automotive sector is mediocre concerning the profitability of the stock exchanges.

Concerning the ownership structure, the situation is practically the same as that of Ford. Just over 1% of shareholders own more than 50% of the shares and the values they represent. The concentration of powerful shareholders influences the board and makes fundamental strategic decisions in the hands of a few and giant financial groups, which invest in thousands of other stocks in various segments of the economy.

The equity acquisitions showed the same movements at Ford, whose shareholders who acquired more shares in 2015 were banks, investment funds, insurance companies and other financial organisations, reinforcing our initial suspicion that these equity movements boosted financialisation.

When we analysed the origins of the directors of General Motors, we saw that most of the executives participated in other boards of directors of financial companies, having a long relationship with the culture of financialisation. Not only do they participate or have participated in banks and other funds, but also in huge companies that maintain the same posture of dependence on financial capital in the business world.

On the issue of dividend payments to shareholders, after starting to make a profit, General Motors sought to allocate most of its net profit to shareholders. It restructured after the 2008/2009 crisis and was rescued by the United States government, which now holds one-third of its controlling interest and sold its stake in 2013. It went from 70% to 78% in 2012, 2013 and 2014, to 100% of its net profit to shareholders in 2015. This is a clear adherence to the principles of MSV, which are controversial, but perfectly recognised and recurrent in the largest businesses, finances or production.

Officers' compensation follows the same pattern as Ford and fulfils criteria present in the largest companies, whose revenues exceeded US$30 billion per year, according to Fortune magazine. It is a set of fixed salaries, short- and long-term shares, bonuses and other incentives that remunerate executives in millions of dollars per year, making them super-executives. The compensations combine the efforts and personal goals of the executives, in addition to other company objectives, such as EBIT, product quality, market share, among others, and reward partly in a fixed way, partly in a variable way, the efforts and risks that each year the company and its professionals face.

Employee salaries are comparable to Ford's, as the lowest, both at Ford and General Motors, are below the average US wage level for all ethnic groups in 2014, according to the US Census Bureau. It is only when you move up the ladder that engineers and managers begin to level up, on average two to three times more than the average American national wage.

When we analyse the differences between the CEO and the other employees, the large division of earnings is evident. As at Ford, at General Motors the CEO earns more than 600 times what an employee with less skills, such as an automotive service technician, earns. This is, for us and a large number of scholars, one of the most striking characteristics of financialisation, the widening inequality of wage incomes.

To summarise the case of General Motors, all of our concerns are described in the tables and texts throughout the pages of this book. They debate the present and the future of the company, which is experiencing an accelerated financialisation process. In the United States, financialisation is classic in the sense that all variables meet the precepts of reducing fixed assets and the growth of financial assets, in addition to the profits from financial activities being higher than those from productive activities; compensations to executives are at millionaire levels; the wages of most workers are more stagnant than in other countries and lower than the average wages of the American population; and dividend payments to shareholders, which reached 100% in several years, drain the entire net profit. Nevertheless, all the variables studied here were found at Ford and General Motors and were fully realised.

This does not imply that financialisation is an exclusively Anglo-Saxon phenomenon, but rather an ideology and an economic movement, which involves material interests, towards capital appreciation through financial activities, thus acquiring different features, depending on the socio-cultural context in which it develops. We will see in the other three automakers that financialisation presents contradictions and a less linear development than in the North American cases studied here.

Hyundai

The financialisation process that takes place at Hyundai has very different characteristics from that of the other automakers, the North American ones studied so far. Although there are also many similarities. Apparently, due to its character as the newest company to enter the market among the five largest automakers studied in this work (Ford, 1903; General Motors, 1909; Volkswagen, 1937; Toyota, 1937 and Hyundai, 1967), but also for its character of family-type conglomerate with a long history of intertwining with the South Korean state, which is highly dependent on it, but also on the foreign market, in which it has managed to increase its participation extraordinarily.

Being younger, more dependent on the state and being a chaebol (family conglomerate) certainly gave a different configuration to the financialisation process, although these facts may also have facilitated Hyundai's adherence to financialisation as there were not so many roots to preserve itself from the previous way of life.

It turns out that the first category studied by us, however, shows a similar movement between the numbers of Hyundai and the numbers of North American automakers, Ford and General Motors. In the three companies, the profitability of financial activities is greater than the profitability of productive activities. Hyundai's productive sector has an average profit lower than its financial subdivisions.

This situation, which leads to the intensification of the exploitation of financial activities and "products", at Hyundai proved to be even more intense than at Ford and General Motors. In North America, there is a financial division that operates all types of financial services, such as leasing and other financings, functioning as banks, but apparently focused on financing the cars sold, that is, directly related to the main activity of the automaker. In Hyundai, there is a division that is divided into Hyundai Card, Capital, Life and Commercial, four subdivisions that explore a wider range of financial products, such as mortgages and life insurance, in addition to loans and credit cards, since the end of the 1990s (Hyundai Card and Hyundai Capital, 2005, p.16). Since 1967, with the arrival of the Diners Club Card in South Korea, coinciding with the founding of Hyundai Motors, there has been a partnership in the exploration of this instrument typical of banks and financial institutions that Hyundai's South Koreans have probably known before even its North American competitors.

Regarding the shareholding composition, we see in Hyundai a concentration of the ten largest shareholders similar to the case of the North American ones, reaching almost 50% of the total shares, but with the difference that from these ten largest shareholders, in Hyundai only five are financial institutions and five are companies of the Hyundai group, in addition to the president and vice president. At Ford and GM, the top ten shareholders are either powerful banks or investment funds, with little representation of the Ford family, for example, which is very different from the case of Hyundai, where the Chung family holds a significant share of power in the company.

The origin of the leaders shows a restricted number of members of the Chung family, composed of a father, son, son-in-law and brother-in-law. Most of these executives had their trajectory in the conglomerate itself, being typically men of the industry, although with doubtful knowledge in each sector of activity, according to critics. In addition to them, five external directors come from the economic, marketing and legal sectors of South Korean society, influential and expressive people who aim to give a sense of security and legitimacy to the business, which has never been well regarded by the international stock market, by stock exchanges values, precisely because of transparency problems (Noble, 2010, p.14).

Dividend payments to shareholders have been increasing, as we saw earlier. They went from 6% in 2012 to 17% in 2015, almost three times more in percentage terms distributed to shareholders, even with a drop in net profit of 39% in those same four years. It is proof of the commitment that Hyundai has with its institutional and foreign investors, increasingly present in the shareholding structure, with a 40% stake in the company's shares. Compared to Ford and General Motors, which have distributed 70% to 100% of their net profit to shareholders over the past four years, Hyundai's dividend payment policy is timid and moderate, marking its already described nature, of a chaebol, with all the peculiarities that allow us to affirm that the financialisation process at Hyundai was late and different from its analysed North American counterparts.

When we refer to the payment of compensation to the executives, we see similarities with the reality of the North Americans. In 2014, the CEO received more than US$12 million for his participation in three companies of the Hyundai Group conglomerate. This value is in line with the earnings of the CEOs of the largest automakers worldwide, with the exception of Toyota, as we will see below. It is even at the same level as the salaries of the managers of the 500 largest companies listed on the S&P 500, an average of US$12 million in 2012, but a far cry from the average earnings of the managers of the largest South Korean companies, which was only US$600,000 in 2012.

In the indicator of salaries paid to employees, we saw that Hyundai has a level similar to that of its North American competitors, although with higher salaries in the case of the assembler than in GM and Ford, at least in the United States. However, when we look at engineers' salaries in South Korea, they are lower than the same jobs in the United States. Within Hyundai itself there are salary differences for the same position depending on the country the company is in. These differences, however, are not the focus of our work at this time. The focus here is to demonstrate the huge disparity between the CEO's earnings and most workers' wages, regardless of the factory.

The differences are striking. They reach more than 500 times the total earnings of the CEO compared to the simplest worker, who earns from 9 to 10 dollars an hour. On average 222 times more than an assembler at the Alabama plant in the United States, who makes $26 an hour. Even compared to a mechanical engineer working in India, for example, the difference between the CEO's earnings for that worker reached 125 times. This is a scenario that practically equates Hyundai with the other automakers, as we have seen in the case of the North American ones and in the cases of Toyota and Volkswagen.

Toyota

One of the main characteristics of financialisation at Toyota is that it mixes elements typical of highly financialised companies (Ford and General Motors) with less financialised companies, such as Hyundai.

When we compare profitability, we see in Toyota the same degree of difference between production profits and profits from financial activities that we find at Ford and General Motors, but not so much at Hyundai and even less at Volkswagen, as we will see below. At Toyota, the differences in profitability are large, as they are proportionately greater in financial activities than in productive activities. While in the last six years the average profit before tax in Toyota's productive sector was 3.6%, in the financial sector of the automaker the average profit before tax was 24.5%. It is a huge difference, and very similar to the situation at Ford and GM. Although the contribution of the productive area is massively higher in absolute numbers, when we analyse the percentages on each revenue, we find an enormous superiority of the financial sector over the productive sector.

In terms of shareholding composition, Toyota outperforms its competitors in terms of financialisation. From the ten largest shareholders, six are banks and two brokers, with only two major shareholders left from the industrial area. Even at General Motors and Ford, where there are powerful financial groups among the largest shareholders, they are funds that invest preferentially in large manufacturing companies. At Toyota, banks account for nearly a third of the shares and are 60% among the top ten shareholders.

Equity acquisitions also followed the path of acquisitions by North American automakers. It was mainly the banks that acquired Toyota shares.

In the category that analysed the origin of the company's directors, we saw a different scenario from that seen at Ford and General Motors. In North America, the leaders had mostly worked at financial institutions before joining the automakers. At Toyota, virtually no manager has worked for finance companies and all are engineers, physicists, economists or lawyers, such as the CEO, Akio Toyoda, who has a law degree. This industrial origin did not, however, prevent them from applying the policy of maximising shareholder value in recent years.

The issue of payment of dividends to shareholders reflected what we have just said. In just four years, Toyota distributed nearly US$50 billion in dividends, which represented 100% of net income. That is, the maximisation of shareholder value has been practised to the letter by executives who came from the industrial world, and this origin has not prevented them from doing so. Officers' compensation proved to be lower than in all the other four automakers studied. They were three to four times lower than those practised by other automakers. They must meet different criteria that deserve to be studied in the future.

Employee salaries showed a variation according to the country where the company is located. They were lower in Japan than in the United States, for example, as demonstrated by the comparison between the salary of the same engineer in the United States and Japan, with an advantage for the professional who works at the Toyota plant in the United States. As the compensation to the CEO is much less at Toyota than that of his/her colleagues from competing automakers, the difference between the number of times between the CEO's total earnings and the salary of the least paid worker is also much less than in the other automakers studied here.

In the case of employment levels at Toyota, the Japanese automaker has been increasing its workforce by considerable levels. It hired more than 25% of its workforce from 2006 to 2016. There were more than 60 thousand new workers hired in a decade. Here, financialisation is also different from the North American process because there was no destruction of fixed assets, but an expansion, since more hired workers also demand new factories and other facilities, in addition to greater material resources and inputs, contrary to what has been occurring with its North American competitors, and similar to its German rival, where we can see that Volkswagen is the company that has further expanded its base of workers and its activities outside Europe.

Volkswagen

The German automaker is one of the giants of the automotive sector, rivalling for some years with the Japanese Toyota automaker to occupy the first position in the ranking of the largest automobile producer. It remains steadfast in the struggle to maintain its market share at around 10% and has not made any losses since 2000, as shown by the series used in this work.

Regarding the differences between the profitability of the automotive sector and the financial sector of each company, Volkswagen is very different from the other four. Its profitability shows similar results, remaining at the same level as single digits. Between 2010 and 2015, the average return on revenue was 4.5% in the automotive sector and 7.5% in the financial sector. Even if the percentages are approximate, there is an advantage for the profitability of the financial sector over the productive sector also at Volkswagen. Here the law of financialisation seems to prevail. This is a trend of contemporary capitalism, that is, the profits from financial activities tend to be greater than the profits from productive activities.

Even at Volkswagen, where the difference is much smaller than in the other four automakers (including Hyundai, which averages 10% in the automotive sector and 19% in the financial, commercial sector), the financial sector, which yielded an average of 7.5%, is 70% higher than the profits of the company's productive sector (average of 4.5% per year).

In the analysis category that discussed the shareholding composition, it is also evident that Volkswagen is different from North American and Japanese Toyota automakers. In these, the main and largest shareholders are banks and financial institutions. The main shareholders are Porsche, which is an industrial company, and the state of Lower Saxony, a state of the German federation. The two together hold 72% of the voting rights and can dominate their decisions.

This did not prevent the MSV from being followed to the letter by the German automaker. Between 97% and 99% of net profit was distributed by the company to shareholders in recent years. More than €57 billion (US$62 billion) was distributed to shareholders in four years, from 2012 to 2015.

Compensation to executives followed the pattern of North American automakers, also practised by Hyundai. Volkswagen's CEO earned more than €15 million in 2014 (US$19.5 million), similar to Ford's Mark Fields (US$18 million) and General Motors' Mary Barra (US$16 million), in addition to Mong-Koo Chung, from Hyundai (US$12 million).

Meanwhile, employees' salaries also allegedly followed the larger law of the economy, which is supply and demand, with different values for equal positions in different countries where the automakers are installed. Each automaker followed the cultural standards and economic dictates of the markets in which they operate. Add to that the exchange rate issue that affects countries differently, the values varied from place to place.

Despite this difference between wages in the various factories that Volkswagen owns in the world, when we look at the comparison between the earnings of the CEO and that of the less-skilled workers, we see a difference that can reach 821 times the earnings of the chief executive compared to that of the workers. At Volkswagen, internal wage inequality is large, caused by high total CEO earnings compared to average wages for the rest of the employees.

However, when compared to the salary inequalities of the North Americans, Volkswagen is halfway between Toyota, less unequal, passing by Hyundai, with a considerable degree of inequality and reaching Ford and General Motors, which are champions in salary difference between the CEO and the rest of the workers.

In terms of employment, Volkswagen differed from the North American Ford and General Motors, which have destroyed jobs over the past few decades. It also distanced itself from the automakers Hyundai and Toyota, which, while creating jobs, went at a much slower pace than the German automaker. This is an aspect that we highlighted at the beginning. Financialisation in non-Anglo-Saxon countries is less intense when it comes to jobs, perhaps because automakers outside the United States are now seeking to occupy the position of largest employers, previously held by United States automakers and are doing so through joint ventures in partnership with Volkswagen, for example. And because maybe that is necessary to stay on top of the biggest automakers in the world. In practice, employment has been changing locations.

This research work provided several findings in the study of the financialisation of the automotive sector. When we launched the categories of analysis that sought to materialise the economic phenomenon of financialisation and confronted them with the empirical data observed, a finding came to light: all initial suspicions were confirmed, although not in a linear manner and without contradictions, but a rich and full of specificities, as we have seen throughout the text.

The comparison between the sources of profitability, the first category of analysis, was found in the literature through the study by Froud et al. (2006). In this study, the authors compared the profits from productive activities with the profits from financial activities at the Ford Motor Company, researching what was the contribution of each sector to the company, from 1988 to 2003. We continued to research these numbers and advanced from 2004 to 2018. We expanded to the five largest automakers today. What we found was an enormous superiority of the profits obtained by the financial activities in opposition to the profits of the productive activities. Table 9.1 shows this difference.

First, we see that the companies with the lowest profitability in the productive sector are Ford and General Motors, but also Volkswagen. They receive around 5% each. Its financial sector, on the other hand, has pre-tax profits ranging from 13% to 37%. Hyundai is the automaker with the highest profit before tax in the production sector compared to the other four. They ranged between 9% and 13.4%. Its financial sector did not perform as well as the productive sector, remaining between 10% and 16%. Volkswagen is the company, of the five, that has the most similar performance between the productive sector and the financial sector, although the latter was slightly above the former, around 8%, twice the average profitability of the productive sector for the period from 2012 to 2015.

Table 9.1 Comparison between the sources of profitability

in %	Ford	General Motors	Hyundai	Toyota	Volkswagen
2012					
Automotive sector	4.7	4.7	12.36	0.12	5.73
Financial sector	25	37.9	16.48	27.84	7.98
2013					
Automotive sector	3.8	5.0	13.39	4.62	5.6
Financial sector	22	26.9	16.29	26.97	8.46
2014					
Automotive sector	1.9	3.7	11.15	8.15	7.22
Financial sector	21	16.6	10.86	20.74	8.06
2015					
Automotive sector	5.8	6.8	9.19	9.27	–1.97
Financial sector	22	13	12.62	21.77	7.94

Source: Automakers' annual reports.

When we look at Toyota, we have fluctuating differences from year to year. Profits before taxes in the company's productive sector are similar to those of Hyundai, around 9%, but in 2012 it fell to 0.12%, while the financial area made a profit before tax of 27.84%. Even after the recovery in 2013, 2014 and 2015, the profit in the productive area was 4%, 8% and 9% respectively, while the profit in the financial area was 26%, 20% and 21%, also respectively. These are levels similar to those of Ford and General Motors, but with higher levels, at Toyota, both in the productive and financial areas.

If we take the four-year average data, from 2012 to 2015, we will see that the profitability generated by financial activities is much higher than that created by productive activities. Figure 9.1 shows the averages, and the result is that at Ford, General Motors and Toyota, the profitability of the financial sector is at least four times greater than the profitability of the automotive sector. At Hyundai, the sources of profitability are approximate: 11% in the productive sector in the average of these four years and 14% in the financial sector of the automaker. Volkswagen is the one with the lowest profits, both in the productive sector and in the financial sector, with an average of 4.14% in the productive sector and 8.11% in the financial sector, although almost double and representing an advantage for the company's financial area.

These figures demonstrate that the studies by Froud et al. (2006) were in the right direction, seeking to unravel the contribution of each sector

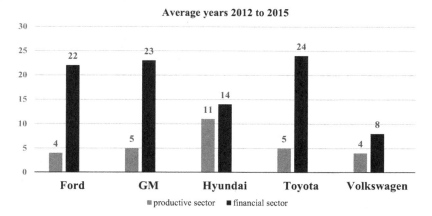

Figure 9.1 Comparison between the sources of profitability by sector, in %
Source: authors, based on the automakers' annual reports.

in the profitability of the business and explaining the increasing dependence of the company for financial activities. The cross-subsidy made by Ford, but also by all others is the recognition that the financial sector is increasingly important, and this has been neglected by several authors, according to Froud et al. (2006). We hope that our research contributes more to the knowledge of this aspect of financialisation.

However, the aspect that draws the most attention to financialisation is the maximisation of shareholder value (MSV). Even more so than the comparison between the sources of profitability, which can induce the recognition of financialisation that is not very detached from production, because it depends on it to create cash flow. It is in the distribution of this net profit that the most determinant aspect of the power of the investors lies. According to Ismail Erturk (2015), what most characterises financialisation is the pursuit of MSV. According to him, even the banks have surrendered to financialisation, making it clear that such an economic movement was not and is not natural, but a product of decisions and a product created and sold by consulting firms and mainstream finance books to be implemented by managers (Erturk, 2015, p.3).

Table 9.2 shows the number of funds that were distributed to shareholders in a very short period, just four years from 2012 to 2015.

Table 9.2 shows that Ford and Toyota have been distributing 100% of net income to shareholders for the past four years. GM moved from

116   *Conclusions*

Table 9.2 % of net profit distributed to shareholders and the total distributed

Automakers	2012	2013	2014	2015	2012–2015 in billions of US$
Ford	100	100	100	100	26,170
General Motors	78	70	71	100	21,120
Hyundai	6,1	6,3	11,1	16,82	2,669
Toyota	100	100	100	100	49,488
Volkswagen	97,5	99,2	99,1	98	62,0

Source: Annual reports of the assemblers and Nasdaq, 2016e,g.

70% to 100% in that period. Volkswagen also almost distributed all net income in that short term, between 97.5% and 99.1% distributed in dividends. The only major automaker company that distributed relatively little of its net profit in dividends was Hyundai, which varied between 6% and 16%, although this indicates a growth of almost 300% in just four years, which highlights the issue that the pressure for an ever-greater return to shareholders begins to show signs of life also in the South Korean company.

These data empirically prove what has been debated in the literature on the subject, basically that developed by William Lazonick. This renowned American author is a staunch critic of the principle of MSV, having written several articles analysing this practice. In one of his texts, he explains how North American corporations transformed from producers to predators (2012, pp.1–6). According to him, the 459 companies listed on the S&P 500 distributed (2001–2010) US$1.9 trillion in dividends in just ten years, equivalent to 40% of their net profit and US$2.6 trillion in share repurchases, and the others 54% of their net profit. He asks: "After all, what was left over for investments in innovation, including upgrading the capabilities of their workforces? Not much" (Lazonick, 2012, p.4).

In another study, Lazonick (2011) analyses how maximising shareholder value robs workers and taxpayers, as it uses all government public resources in support of research and development in the area of health and medicine, for example, to later privatise profits and distribute in the form of dividends and share buybacks. Finally, Lazonick (2013) states that "robots do not destroy jobs, but rapacious executives from corporations do".

That is, we have here the theoretical confirmation, coming from a great scholar on the subject, that financialisation, from the domination of the investors, and the application of the principle of MSV, are

Table 9.3 Compensations to the Chief Executive Officers – 2014

	CEO	US$
Ford	Mark Fields	18,596,497
General Motors	Mary Barra	16,162,828
Hyundai	Mong Koo Chung	12,269,937
Toyota	Akio Toyoda	2,840,000
Volkswagen	Martin Winterkorn	19,509,617

Source: Annual reports from automakers.

products of decisions taken by the high executives and shareholders at meetings and boards of directors, for which material interests are defined in an alliance, which involves the payment of dividends to shareholders and the millionaire compensation to executives. In Table 9.3 we see this aspect of financialisation, which is the creation of a layer of highly paid executives, whose compensation is very different from the salaries of the remaining workers, as we saw in the tables that compared the salaries of employees and the earnings of CEOs.

Regarding the remuneration of top executives, a comparison between Ford, General Motors, Hyundai and Volkswagen can be observed in Table 9.3. Toyota is left out in this regard because it was the automaker that paid the least compensation to its executives, including CEO Akio Toyoda. The other four automakers, in turn, followed the pattern of the largest companies in the world, whether financial or not, and paid substantial compensation to their managers, uniting executives and shareholders in a new alliance that represents a new moment, following the shareholders' revolution. This new moment marks the support and adherence to financialisation.

The other categories of analysis also corroborated our initial suspicions. Ownership control has shown that large banks and financial institutions are increasingly holding shareholder rights and increasingly have influence over automakers. The acquisitions also showed that banks and other financial groups were the ones that most acquired shares in the auto companies, increasing their control over them.

The origin of the leaders showed two things. That in some companies (Ford and General Motors, mainly) the main leaders passed through the world of finance before entering the administration of the assembly companies. This seems normal in terms of corporate control, as pointed out by Fligstein (1990), but this does not seem to be a *conditio sine qua non* for the sanction of MSV, since other automakers, such as Volkswagen and Toyota, have among their leaders the vast majority of engineers and other professionals from the factory world, which did not prevent them from making decisions equal to those of their finance colleagues, distributing almost all of the net profit to shareholders. That is, the financialised mentality ends up reaching all large companies, regardless of where their leadership comes from. It is the strength of what Lazonick and O'Sullivan (2000, p.13) called the true ideology of the corporate world.

The financialisation process of the automotive sector has been developing for at least 25 years, depending on the automaker. American automakers are pioneers, even though they are older. Toyota comes next, as it has had banks and financial institutions among its shareholders for a long time. At Volkswagen, this process faced greater resilience, as demonstrated by Kädtler and Sperling (2002), due to its shareholding structure, which has as its largest shareholder Porsche, an industrial company and the state of Lower Saxony, that is, a unit of the German federation, which must be accountable to citizens and is presumed to take into account interests other than profit. However, only four years of data showed that even at Volkswagen, the resilience of operations meant a gradual adaptation to the new times. Lastly, we consider Hyundai to be the least financialised, in general because it was the youngest to enter the automotive industry, among the five assemblers studied, and its financialisation process can be considered late, but it does not exist for that reason.

Here, there is a distinction in the financialisation process of the automakers. Although corporate financial services make proportionately higher profits than manufacturing, these services indeed depend on the sphere of production, they depend on automobiles being produced to be sold in a financed manner, in the manner of banks and credit institutions. This could indicate that financialisation in the automakers is not so detached from the productive sphere, as it would only be an extension of sales activities, but it is not quite so.

When we see that compensation to executives includes stock options, a mechanism that aims to pay executives through company shares and thereby increases the price of shares, artificially, therefore, we note that we have the classic capital-money formula that self-values without going through the sphere of production, M-M′ (money that generates more money), as demonstrated in the work of Chesnais (1996, p.290). That is, financialisation affects automakers in more ways than one. First, because it has proportionally higher profits in financial activities, and second, because production fuels financialisation through the payment of dividends to shareholders, which drains almost all the net profit of the analysed automakers.

Final considerations

We were able to conclude with our work that the *raison d'être* of production seems, today, to satisfy the interests of finance. We seek to contribute to the research agenda on financialisation in general and the automotive sector in particular. We hope to have helped in the construction of empirical knowledge and in strengthening the theoretical constructs of economic sociology, which seeks to study economic phenomena with the help of an interdisciplinary tool, joining various sciences for a better understanding of society and the economy.

We use five cases of automakers that are at the top of the largest automobile producers worldwide. Much of the data in companies' annual reports has been changed over time. The requirements for transparency, disclosure and compliance increasingly expand the amount of data available. However, not everything is widely publicised. One of the problems of this work was with obtaining data about the Hyundai automaker. In the case of compensation to Hyundai managers, the information was revealed for the first time recently, in 2014, and even so in a limited way. The same happened with information about the number of workers, which at Hyundai is still incomplete. We were unable to produce a large historical series that demonstrates the evolution of employment at Hyundai. We only obtained data for six years, which is good for our work.

Other data are also subject to adjustments from one year to the next, changing the information contained in the previous year's report. Not all automakers have their annual report according to the North American standards required by the Securities and Exchange Commission (SEC), which greatly facilitates the identification of data and information, standardising documents.

Greater ease in obtaining data over the Internet was essential for the progress of the work, without which we would not be able to research without leaving the country or by other non-electronic means. This will favour that more researchers can adhere to this research agenda. An agenda that grows every day, with theorists and scholars of financialisation moving into the most diverse sectors of society and the economy, trying to understand what financialisation is and how it happens, opening up a whole debate on this important theme nowadays.

Regarding the personal impressions of the authors, the study on financialisation in the automotive sector revealed several surprises. Using a basic analysis procedure in the social sciences, which is that which endeavours to establish similarities and differences, continuities and discontinuities in a social process, our study ended up showing that financialisation happens differently in different countries where the companies we analysed are based, without corroborating that financialisation would be an Anglo-Saxon process *par excellence*. For us, it is not.

Indeed, the theoretical production that calls for financialisation and MSV is much more developed in the United States and the United Kingdom, but the ideology will arrive everywhere sooner or later, albeit unevenly and with different rhythms, depending on the dimension analysed.

In the case of managers at Hyundai, for example, which is a family business, executive compensation is several million dollars a year, very similar to Ford and GM, companies native to the United States, and very similar also to the German Volkswagen. In the Japanese Toyota, the remuneration for managers is three to four times lower than in the other four automakers analysed. What does that mean? Does any specific cultural issue in Japan impose a lower remuneration on its leaders even though Toyota is the largest producer of automobiles and the automaker with the highest revenue and net profit in 2014 and 2015 among all the world's automakers? Has it always been like that? Our study did not provide all of these answers, since that was not our initial intention, as it is still an exploratory study. But these are questions that can and should be addressed in more depth in future research.

What else is Hyundai similar to with Ford and General Motors, other than the issue of compensation to managers? Dividend payments to shareholders is quite different for the time being. In the United States, the order is 80 to 100% of net income paid in the form of dividends. In South Korea, this amount is much lower, ranging from 6% in 2012 to 16% in 2015. However, this jump of almost 300% in the amount of resources distributed in just four years and the promise made by Hyundai to increase to 20%, 25% and then 35% of the distributed net profit (until reaching higher levels) implies that the commitment to maximise shareholder value is also present in the South Korean automaker, which enters the club of the big and old automakers in this regard, although it is a company younger than the American ones. The employment issue reveals differences between Ford, General Motors and Hyundai. Although Hyundai has grown in number of workers, and General Motors and Ford have decreased their employment levels, it has been a light, continuous and less abrupt growth than Volkswagen, for example. However, one thing Hyundai and the other four are in agreement on is: jobs start to grow outside South Korea, indicating that the search for cheaper labour and abundant natural resources guides both North Americans, Asians, as well as Europeans. In this search for cheaper foreign production, all automakers are alike.

Analysing these similarities and differences shows much intellectual prejudice towards the United States, the biggest capitalist country today, as if it were sinfully adhering to financialisation, while in other places, such as in continental Europe (France and Germany mainly) with its social economies and market coordinates, the watchword would be the full respect for the people and not the exclusive pursuit of profit. This is partly true, as Europeans have traditionally shown a greater concern for the welfare state and equality, much greater than the Americans. Notably Americans, apparently value freedom more (and here the main one seems to be the freedom of private initiative) than equality.

However, despite this debate about political philosophy conceptions involving each country and each culture, when we see that in German Volkswagen the value of net profit distributed to shareholders reached more than 97% in just four years, draining almost all net profit, it is questionable how a central category of financialisation can occur so strongly in a country that practices a welfare state, a social market economy and propagates, through its national authors, the resilience of operations in the face of financialisation.

The occurrence of such resilience is also true, since at Volkswagen, when talking about employment, there were more than 50% of hires in the last ten years, while at Ford and General Motors, there was a decrease between 50% and 60%, respectively, in the productive force over the last two decades. In this regard, employment, financialisation was not cruel at Volkswagen, although we remember that half of the current 600,000 employees of the German automaker are outside Germany, much of it in joint ventures in China. This is another contradictory aspect of financialisation. Does it destroy jobs or just move them?

If Germany advocates the welfare state and this is reflected in the policy of its companies, the automakers do not seem to follow all the guiding principles to the letter. Let us remember that the scandal of emissions in diesel vehicles happened very recently. Lying, disguising, even circumventing the fight for a cleaner, less polluting and sustainable automobile industry, just to earn more, to profit more, was a conduct that left an indelible stain on the brand image and put the supreme honesty, rigidity and German seriousness at stake.

When we refer to the salary level, we are aware that the wages paid in Germany are higher than those paid in other countries. This is one of the classic logics of financialisation, redirecting production geographically to reduce costs in any way, thereby expanding the payment of dividends to shareholders. Germany has been adhering to this mentality and that is what we have been able to verify at least in the four years analysed, at Volkswagen, as our research has shown.

In general, jobs in the United States and Western Europe, which are more expensive, are sacrificed to increase the labour force, which is almost always cheaper, in other countries. In a general scenario, the same number of workers in the automakers can still be seen today as there have been in the past ten years, having decreased in some places and increased in others, but their wages certainly decreased (another point that deserves investigation), since the geographical changes in production meet this need for lower wages and natural resources that are easy to find and also cheaper, providing huge savings in production costs.

This debate is at the centre of attention today and was evident in the US presidential elections in 2016. The winner, Donald Trump, was victorious mostly because of dissatisfaction with traditional politics and the establishment, caused by the critical situation of an immense working class that had millions of jobs cut (and automakers were responsible for significant plant cuts and closings) and transferred to China, India, Malaysia, Indonesia, Eastern Europe, among other destinations that made it possible for North American automakers to form strategic alliances in these countries and thus increase their competitive advantages among all global competitors.

Here other issues emerge. How can the institutions in each country influence the situation caused by globalisation, which has transferred many jobs from the United States and Europe, to Asia, Southeast Asia and Eastern Europe? A "disruptive" policy by former President Trump in the United States has not taken place in a way that will be able to return the millions of jobs lost at United States and foreign automakers operating in the country. Would it be possible to stop the force of globalisation and the internationalisation of capital, information and flows of goods and services that characterise the current era? And is this what is needed to make the capitalism of the future better for more people?

Likewise, would it be possible for countries, through their legal statutes, to impose severe impediments to the free payment of dividends to shareholders, which drain almost all of the net profit? Could the tax codes intercede for the regulation of profit sharing or is this an act of exclusive interplay between the participants? The political, social, legal and economic spheres show their interpenetration and extreme influence that one has over the other.

Finally, as seen in the work of Van der Zwan (2014), more research must be carried out to account for such a complex phenomenon. Whether it is a new mode of accumulation, the rise of a new orientation aimed at maximising shareholder value or the financialisation of everyday life, all these dimensions deserve further study and, if it depends on us, we will always be ready to contribute with this important research agenda.

Afterword

by *Raphael Jonathas da Costa Lima*

While this book was being finalised, Ford Motor Company was in the process of restructuring its global operations having a direct impact on emerging countries, such as Brazil. The company has drawn up a strategy to change its business model directly appealing to Sport Utility Vehicles (SUVs), a vehicle model that has become increasingly important for many automakers' sales strategies due to its high aggregate value. Moreover, a quick, disruptive process is taking place in the sector as electric vehicles are replacing combustion engines, autonomous vehicles are being developed to be used mainly for services, and automobile groups' businesses are expanding beyond production and selling products. Therefore, multinational companies, such as Ford, have been endeavouring to ensure the viability of their businesses, taking risks to diversify their portfolios in after-sales services (spare parts, for example), car rental and even insurance sales.

Taking this into account, those who keep up with trends in the sector were not surprised by this move initiated by the North American automaker in 2019 when it gradually started downsizing its line-up, and consequently staff in the country, closing its traditional truck plant in São Bernardo do Campo in the state of São Paulo. Two years later, its manufacturing operations ceased as the company closed three more factories. Ford simply ended a cycle that had started in 1919 when it began importing Lincoln vehicles to sell in Brazil. Altogether all the Ford units in Brazil directly employed around 7,000 workers. In order to have a bigger picture of what this exactly entails in terms of the end of the company's production, it is estimated that the closure of one of its units – the Camaçari plant, in Bahia state – will lead to around 50 thousand employed workers alone being laid off from jobs directly or indirectly related to production.

Ford's departure from Brazil, as well as other countries, has been attributed to numerous reasons, such as the loss of market share in national markets due to its technological backwardness and the difficulty in keeping up with old (General Motors and Volkswagen) and new (Hyundai) competitors. On a global level, various competitors have been revamped to compete with other automakers to obtain a larger share of the market, such as FIAT-Chrysler and PSA Peugeot-Citroën groups when they merged into the Stellantis Group.

However, a hypothesis put forward here, and fulfilling the purpose of this book, aims to relate Ford's corporate strategies of closing industrial plants, discontinuing products and launching others to short-term calculations that seem to have been Ford's *modus operandi* in recent years. As discussed in this book, this is due to the increasing power of controlling investment funds that are less inclined to institutional commitments and the effects of their decisions on emerging countries such as Brazil, which are still very dependent on development programs based on generating many jobs, even precarious ones in robust value chains such as the automobile industry. Considering this, Ford is, and still will be for a long time ahead, an emblematic case of subjecting the automobile sector to purposes of ensuring better conditions of return to its shareholders, thus reinforcing shareholder value maximisation principles.

Raphael Jonathas da Costa Lima
Professor of the Graduate Program in Sociology (PPGS)
Fluminense Federal University (UFF)
Volta Redonda, Rio de Janeiro, Brazil

References

Associação Nacional das Empresas Financeiras das Montadoras (Anef), 2015. São Paulo, Brasil. Available at: www.anef.com.br. Accessed 17 March 2015.

Associação Nacional dos Fabricantes de veículos Automotores (Anfavea), 2015. *Anuário da Indústria Automobilística Brasileira*, São Paulo, Brasil. Available at: www.anfavea.com.br. Accessed 28 February 2016.

Bailey, D., Ruyter, A., Michie, J. and Tyler, P., 2010. Global restructuring and the auto industry. *Cambridge Journal of Regions, Economy and Society*, 3, pp. 311–318.

Bebchuk, L.A. and Fried, J.M, 2004. *Pay without Performance. The Unfulfilled Promise of Executive Compensation, Part II: Power and Pay,* (draft of the book, Pay without Performance, The Unfulfilled Promise of Executive Compensation, Harvard University Press). Available at: www.law.harvard.edu/faculty/bebchuk/pdfs/Performance-Part2.pdf. Accessed 28 February 2016.

Boyer, R., 2005. From shareholder value to CEO power: The paradox of the 1990´s. *PSE Working Paper*, No. 2005-10. Available at: https://halshs.archives-ouvertes.fr/halshs-00590848/document. Accessed 28 February 2016.

Boyer, R. and Freyssenet, M., 2000. *Les modèles productifs*. Découverte, Paris, Repères, La.

BlackRock, Inc., 2019. Introduction to BlackRock. Available at: www.blackrock.com/sg/en/introduction-to-blackrock. Accessed 20 January 2020.

Bloomberg, 2015. Available at: www.bloomberg.com. Accessed 30 July 2015.

Careerbliss, 2016. Hyundai Motors Assembly Line Worker Salaries. Available at: www.careerbliss.com/hyundai-motors/salaries/assembly-line-worker/. Accessed 7 September 2016.

Casotti, B. P. and Goldenstein, M., 2008. Panorama do Setor Automotivo: As Mudanças Estruturais da Indústria e as Perspectivas para o Brasil. *BNDES Setorial*, 28, pp. 147–188, Rio de Janeiro.

Chesnais, F., 1996. Os grupos industriais, agentes ativos da mundialização financeira. *A mundialização do Capital*. Editora Xamã, São Paulo.

Cuex, 2016. Conversor de moedas. Available at: https://cuex.com/pt/. Accessed 19 September 2016

Day, G. and Fahey, L., 1990. Putting Strategy into shareholder value analysis. *Harvard Business Review*. From the Magazine (March–April 1990). Available at: https://hbr.org/1990/03/putting-strategy-into-shareholder-value-analysis. Accessed 20 April 2017.

Davis, G. F., 2009. *Managed by the Markets. How Finance Reshaped America.* Oxford University Press.

Davis, G. F. and Kim, S., 2015. Financialization of the Economy. *Annual Review of Sociology*, 41, pp.203–221.

Donadone, J. C. and Matsuda, P. M., 2015. A mudança da carreira dos dirigentes após o processo de privatização: estudo de caso no setor elétrico paulista. *Gestão & Produção*, São Carlos, 22, 2, pp. 419–430.

Dunhaupt, P., 2010. Financialization and rentier income share: evidence from the USA and Germany. *IMK Working Paper*, no. 2/2010. Hans-Böckler-Stiftung, Institut für Makroökonomie und Konjunkturforschung (IMK), Düsseldorf.

Elías, J. C., 2013a. The impact of the variable financialization in the collapse of General Motors Corporation of 2008. Gerpisa colloquium, Paris.

Elías, J. C., 2013b. Análisis de la quiebra de General Motors Corporation de 2008, desde la finaciarización. XVIII Congreso Internacional de Contaduría, Administración e Informática, Ciudad Universitaria, México, D.F.

Elías, J. C., 2014. Financial analysis of the Volkswagen group from financialization point of view (1991–2007). Gerpisa colloquium, Paris.

Elías, J. C and Granados, V.M.A.M. 2015. Toyota Motor Company: desarrollo y crecimiento desde el punto de vista de la financiarización. XX Congreso Internacional de Contaduría, Administración e Informática, Ciudad Universitaria, México, D.F.

Epstein, G., 2002. Financialization, rentier interest, and central bank policy. *Paper prepared for PERI Conference on "Financialization of the World Economy"*, 7–8 December 2001, University of Massachusetts, Amherst. This version, June, 2002.

Erturk, I., 2015. Financialization, bank business models and the limits of post-crisis bank regulation. *Journal of Banking Regulation*. 17, pp. 60–72. Available at: https://link.springer.com/article/10.1057/jbr.2015.23. Accessed 20 April 2017.

Ezzamel, M., Willmott, H. and Worthington, F., 2008. Manufacturing share-holder value: the role of accounting in the organizational transformation. *Accounting, Organizations and Society*. 33, 2–3, pp. 107–140. Available at: www.sciencedirect.com/science/article/abs/pii/S036136820700027X. Accessed on 25 February 2017.

Fantti, M. B. L. and Donadone, J. C., 2020. The influence of the financial logic in the National Quality Award. *Gestão & Produção*, 27, 2, e5052. Available at: doi.org/10.1590/0104-530X5052-20. Accessed 20 April 2017.

Fichtner, J., Heemskerk, E.M. and Garcia-Bernardo, J., 2017. Hidden power of the Big Three? Passive index funds, re-concentration of corporate owner-ship, and new financial risk. *Business and Politics*, 19, 2, pp. 298–326.

Fligstein, N., 1990. *The Transformation of Corporate Control.* Harvard University Press, Cambridge.

Fligstein, N., 1991. The structural transformation of American industry: an institutional account of the causes of diversification in the largest firms, 1919–1979. *The New Institutionalism in Organizational Analysis.* Paul J. DiMaggio and Walter W. Powell (eds.), pp. 311–336. University of Chicago Press, Chicago.

Ford Motor Company, 2002. Ford Motor Company 2002 annual report. Available at: https://shareholder.ford.com/investors/financials-and-filings/default.aspx. Accessed 24 May 2021.

Ford Motor Company, 2003. Ford Motor Company 2003 annual report. Detroit. Available at: https://shareholder.ford.com/investors/financials-and-filings/default.aspx. Accessed 24 May 2021.

Ford Motor Company, 2004. Ford Motor Company 2004 annual report. Detroit. Available at: https://shareholder.ford.com/investors/financials-and-filings/default.aspx. Accessed 24 May 2021.

Ford Motor Company, 2005. Ford Motor Company 2005 annual report. Detroit. Available at: https://shareholder.ford.com/investors/financials-and-filings/default.aspx. Accessed 24 May 2021.

Ford Motor Company, 2006. Ford Motor Company 2006 annual report. Detroit. Available at: https://shareholder.ford.com/investors/financials-and-filings/default.aspx. Accessed 24 May 2021.

Ford Motor Company, 2007. Ford Motor Company 2007 annual report. Detroit. Available at: https://shareholder.ford.com/investors/financials-and-filings/default.aspx. Accessed 24 May 2021.

Ford Motor Company, 2008. Ford Motor Company 2008 annual report. Detroit. Available at: https://shareholder.ford.com/investors/financials-and-filings/default.aspx. Accessed 24 May 2021.

Ford Motor Company, 2009. Ford Motor Company 2009 annual report. Detroit. Available at: https://shareholder.ford.com/investors/financials-and-filings/default.aspx. Accessed 24 May 2021.

Ford Motor Company, 2010. Ford Motor Company 2010 annual report. Detroit. Available at: https://shareholder.ford.com/investors/financials-and-filings/default.aspx. Accessed 24 May 2021.

Ford Motor Company, 2011. Ford Motor Company 2011 annual report. Detroit. Available at: https://shareholder.ford.com/investors/financials-and-filings/default.aspx. Accessed 24 May 2021.

Ford Motor Company, 2012. Ford Motor Company 2012 annual report. Detroit. Available at: https://shareholder.ford.com/investors/financials-and-filings/default.aspx. Accessed 24 May 2021.

Ford Motor Company, 2013. Ford Motor Company 2013 annual report. Detroit. Available at: https://shareholder.ford.com/investors/financials-and-filings/default.aspx. Accessed 24 May 2021.

Ford Motor Company, 2014. Ford Motor Company 2014 annual report. Detroit. Available at: https://s22.q4cdn.com/857684434/files/doc_financials/2014/annual/f-12-31-2014-10-k.pdf. Accessed 30 June 2019.

Ford Motor Company, 2015a. Ford Motor Company 2015 annual report. Detroit. Available at: https://shareholder.ford.com/investors/financials-and-filings/default.aspx. Accessed 24 May 2021.

Ford Motor Company, 2015b. Proxy statement. Available at: https://corporate.ford.com/content/dam/corporate/en/investors/reports-and-filings/Proxy%20Statements/2015-ford-proxy-statement.pdf. Accessed 30 June 2019.

Ford Motor Company, 2016. Ford Motor Company 2016 annual report. www.annualreports.com/HostedData/AnnualReportArchive/f/NYSE_F_2016.pdf. Accessed 20 May 2021.

Ford Motor Company, 2017. Ford Motor Company 2017 annual report. Detroit. Available at: https://shareholder.ford.com/investors/financials-and-filings/default.aspx. Accessed 24 May 2021.

Ford Motor Company, 2018. Ford Motor Company 2018 annual report. Detroit. Available at: https://shareholder.ford.com/investors/financials-and-filings/default.aspx. Accessed 24 May 2021.

Froud, J., Johal, S. and Williams, K., 2002. New agendas for auto research: financialization, motoring and present-day capitalism. *Competition & Change*, 6, 1, pp. 1–11.

Froud, J., Johal, S., Leaver, A. and Williams, K., 2006. *Financialization & Strategy: Narrative and Numbers*. Routledge, England.

Gabriel, L. F., Schneider, A.H., Skrobot, F.C.C. and Souza, M. 2010. Uma análise da indústria automobilística no Brasil e a demanda de veículos automotores: algumas evidências para o período recente. *Área (8) – Economia Industrial e da Tecnologia. Federação das Indústrias do Estado do Paraná – FIEP*.

General Motors Corporation, 2003. Annual Report 2003. Available at: https://www.annualreports.com/HostedData/AnnualReportArchive/g/NYSE_GM_2003.pdf. Accessed 21 May 2021.

General Motors Corporation, 2004. Annual Report 2004. Available at: https://www.annualreports.com/HostedData/AnnualReportArchive/g/NYSE_GM_2004.pdf. Accessed 21 May 2021.

General Motors Corporation, 2005. Annual Report 2005. Available at: https://www.annualreports.com/HostedData/AnnualReportArchive/g/NYSE_GM_2005.pdf. Accessed 21 May 2021.

General Motors Corporation, 2006. Annual Report 2006. Available at: https://www.annualreports.com/HostedData/AnnualReportArchive/g/NYSE_GM_2006.pdf. Accessed 21 May 2021.

General Motors Corporation, 2007. Annual Report 2007. Available at: https://www.annualreports.com/HostedData/AnnualReportArchive/g/NYSE_GM_2007.pdf. Accessed 21 May 2021.

General Motors Corporation, 2008. Annual Report 2008.

General Motors Corporation, 2009. Annual Report 2009. Available at: https://www.annualreports.com/HostedData/AnnualReportArchive/g/NYSE_GM_2009.pdf. Accessed 21 May 2021.

130 *References*

General Motors Corporation, 2010. Annual Report 2010. Available at: https:// www.annualreports.com/HostedData/AnnualReportArchive/g/NYSE_ GM_2010.pdf. Accessed 21 May 2021.

General Motors Corporation, 2011. Annual Report 2011. Available at: https:// www.annualreports.com/HostedData/AnnualReportArchive/g/NYSE_ GM_2011.pdf. Accessed 21 May 2021.

General Motors Corporation, 2012. Annual Report 2012. Available at: https:// www.annualreports.com/HostedData/AnnualReportArchive/g/NYSE_ GM_2012.pdf. Accessed 21 May 2021.

General Motors Corporation, 2013. Annual Report 2013. Available at: https:// www.annualreports.com/HostedData/AnnualReportArchive/g/NYSE_ GM_2013.pdf. Accessed 21 May 2021.

General Motors Corporation, 2014. Annual Report 2014. Available at: https:// www.annualreports.com/HostedData/AnnualReportArchive/g/NYSE_ GM_2014.pdf. Accessed 21 May 2021.

General Motors Corporation, 2015a. Annual Report 2015. Available at: https:// www.annualreports.com/HostedData/AnnualReportArchive/g/NYSE_ GM_2015.pdf. Accessed 21 May 2021.

General Motors Corporation, 2015b. Proxy Statement 2015. Available at: https://investor.gm.com/static-files/8455e5ae-16b3-4ff5-9f78-c81818d16489. Accessed 30 April 2015.

Glassdoor, 2016a. Hyundai Motor South Korea Salaries. Available at: www.glassdoor.com/Salary/Hyundai-Motor-South-Korea-Salaries-EI_ IE7474.0,13_IL.14,25_IN135.htm. Accessed 9 May 2021.

Glassdoor, 2016b. Hyundai Motor China Salaries. Available at: www.glassdoor. com/Salary/Hyundai-Motor-China-Salaries-EI_IE7474.0,13_IL.14,19_ IN48.htm. Accessed 22 March 2016.

Glassdoor, 2016c. Toyota North America Salaries. Available at: www.glassdoor. com/Salary/Toyota-North-America-Salaries-E3544.htm. Accessed 21 May 2021.

Glassdoor, 2016d. Volkswagen China Salaries. Available at: www.glassdoor. com/Salary/Volkswagen-China-Salaries-EI_IE3515.0,10_IL.11,16_IN48. htm. Accessed 22 March 2016.

Glassdoor, 2016e. Toyota North America Japan Salaries. Available at: www.glassdoor.com/Salary/Toyota-North-America-Japan-Salaries-EI_ IE3544.0,20_IL.21,26_IN123.htm. Accessed 22 March 2016

Godechot, O., 2015. Financialization is marketization! A study on the respective impact of various dimensions of financialization on the increase in global inequality. *MaxPo Discussion Paper*, 15/3.

Goutas, L. and Lane, C., 2009. The translation of shareholder value in the German business system: A comparative study of Daimler-Chrysler and Volkswagen AG. *Competition & Change*, 13, 4, pp. 327–346.

Green, A.E., 1992. South Korea's automobile industry: development and prospects. *Asian Survey*, 32, , pp. 411–428. Available at: http://links.jstor.org/ sici?sici=0004-4687%28199205%2932%3A5%3C411%3ASKAIDA%3E2.0. CO%3B2-O. Accessed 17 July 2016.

Guttmann, R., 1999. As mutações do capital financeiro. *A mundialização financeira: gênese, custos e riscos*. François Chesnais (Ed.), Editora Xamã, São Paulo.

Guzman, G., 2017. Household income: 2016. *American Community Survey Briefs*. US Census Bureau. Available at: www.census.gov/content/dam/Census/library/publications/2017/acs/acsbr16-02.pdf. Accessed 9 September 2019.

Hardie, I., 2008. Financialization, loyalty and the rise of short-term shareholder value. ESRC Seminar 'Financialization of Competitiveness', Northumbria University.

Ho, K., 2009. *Liquidated. An Ethnography of Wall Street*. Duke University Press, Durham and London.

Hyundai Card and Hyundai Capital, 2005. Annual Report 2005. Reaching New Heights. Available at: https://total-impact.net/?projects=2005-hyundai-card-capital-annual-report. Accessed 9 July 2016.

Hyundai Motor Company, 2010–2015. Annual reports. Available at: www.hyundai.com/worldwide/en/company/ir/financial-information/financial-statements. Accessed 24 May 2021.

Hyundai Motor Company, 2014. Annual Report. Available at: www.hyundai.com/content/dam/hyundai/ww/en/images/about-hyundai/ir/financial-statements/annual-report/hw103155.pdf. Accessed 21 May 2021.

Hyundai Motor Company, 2016a. Annual Report. Available at: www.hyundai.com/content/dam/hyundai/ww/en/images/about-hyundai/ir/financial-statements/annual-report/HMCAnnualReport20160630.pdf. Accessed 21 December 2016.

Hyundai Motor Company, 2016b. Brief information for shareholders. Available at: www.hyundai.com/worldwide/en/company/ir/corporate-information/bod/shareholders. Accessed 14 September 2016.

Hyundai Motor Company, 2016c. Board of Directors. Available at: www.hyundai.com/worldwide/en/company/ir/corporate-information/bod/board-of-directors. Accessed 21 October 2016.

Hyundai Motor Company, 2016d. Dividend History. Available at: www.hyundai.com/worldwide/en/company/ir/stock-information/dividend-history. Accessed 20 May 2021.

International Labour Organization, 2015. *Global Wage Report 2014/15. Wages and Income Inequality*. International Labour Office, Geneva.

International Organization of Motor Vehicle Manufacturers, OICA, 2014. World Motor Vehicle Production. OICA Correspondents Survey. Available at: www.oica.net/wp-content/uploads//Ranking-2014-Q4-Rev.-22-July.pdf. Accessed 15 March 2015.

International Organization of Automobile Manufacturers, OICA, 2015a. Production data, sales and ranking of automakers, 1998–2014. Available at: www.oica.net. Accessed 2 February 2016. World Ranking of Manufacturers, Year 2014. Available at: www.oica.net/wp-content/uploads//Ranking-2014-Q4-Rev.-22-July.pdf; Year 2015 available at: www.oica.net/wp-content/uploads//ranking2015.pdf

International Organization of Motor Vehicle Manufacturers, OICA, 2015b. World Motor Vehicle Production. OICA Correspondents Survey. Available at: www.oica.net/wp-content/uploads//ranking2015.pdf. Accessed 21 April 2016.

Investing, 2016. Available at: http://br.investing.com/equities/volkswagen-ag. Accessed 2 June 2017.

Jurgens, U., Lung, Y., Volpato, G. and Frigant, V., 2002. The arrival of shareholder value in the European auto industry. A case study comparison of four car makers. *Competition & Change*, 6, 1, pp. 61–80.

Kädtler, J. and Sperling, H.J., 2002. The power of financial markets and the resilience of operations: argument and evidence from the German car industry. *Competition & Change*, 6, 1, pp. 81–94.

Kawano, K., 2019. What is the average salary in Japan in 2019? Available at: https://blog.gaijinpot.com/what-is-the-average-salary-in-japan-in-2019/#:~:text=Which%20jobs%20in%20Japan%20offer,beyond%20the%20Tokyo%202020%20Olympics.&text=The%20average%20annual%20salary%20in,That's%20about%20US%2437%2C800. Accessed 19 June 2019.

Kim, R., 2014. Hyundai Motors reveals chairman's pay for the first time. 31 March 2014. Available at: www.bloomberg.com/news/articles/2014-03-31/hyundai-motor-reveals-chairman-s-pay-for-first-time. Accessed 31 July 2016.

Kroll, L., 2016. Forbes 2016 World's Billionaires: Meet the Richest People on the Planet. 1 March 2016. Available at: www.forbes.com/sites/luisakroll/2016/03/01/forbes-2016-worlds-billionaires-meet-the-richest-people-on-the-planet/?sh=69680a1f77dc. Accessed 10 April 2016.

Kubota, C. T., 2012. O Papel do Banco Toyota na Estratégia da Montadora Toyota-Dissertação de Mestrado em Administração de Empresas –92f., EAESP/FGV, São Paulo, Brazil.

Lazonick, W., 2011. How 'maximizing value' for shareholders robs workers and taxpayers. *Huffpost Business*. Available at: www.huffpost.com/entry/how-maximizing-value-for-_b_892396. Accessed 23 September 2016.

Lazonick, W., 2012. How American corporations transformed from producers to predators. *Huffpost Business*. Available at: www.huffpost.com/entry/how-american-corporations_b_1399500. Accessed 23 September 2016.

Lazonick, W., 2013. Robots don't destroy jobs; rapacious corporate executives do. *Huffpost Business*, Available at: www.huffpost.com/entry/robots-dont-destroy-jobs-_b_2396465. Accessed 23 September 2016.

Lazonick, W. and O'Sullivan, M., 2000. Maximizing shareholder value: a new ideology for corporate governance. *Economy and Society*, 29, 1, pp.13–35.

Lim, Y., 2002. Hyundai Crisis: its development and resolution. Korea Development Institute. *Journal of East Asian Studies*, 2, 1, pp. 261–283. Available at: http://santafemods.com/History/lim2.pdf. Accessed 18 August 2016.

Marketscreener, 2016. Hyundai Motor Company Shareholders. Available at: www.marketscreener.com/quote/stock/HYUNDAI-MOTOR-COMPANY-6492384/company/. Accessed 14 September 2016.

Martins, T. J., 2014. A nova elite financeira no Brasil: jogos, estratégias e disputas entre os 'gerentes-engenheiros' e os acionistas. *Revista de Economia Política e História Econômica*, n° 32.

Maubossin, M., 2011. What Shareholder Value is really about. *Harvard Business Review*. Available at: https://hbr.org/2011/10/ceos-must-understand-what-crea. Accessed 15 October 2016.

Mazzucato, M. 2014. *O Estado empreendedor. Desmascarando o mito do setor público vs. setor privado*. Editora Schwarcz S.A., São Paulo.

Minchington, C. and Francis, G.A., 2000. Shareholder Value. *Management Quarterly*, 6, pp. 23–31.

Moerman, L. C. and Van Der Laan, S., 2007. Pursuing Shareholder Value: The Rhetoric of James Hardie. *Accounting Forum*, 31, 4, pp. 354–369.

Mollo, M. L. R., 2011. Financeirização como desenvolvimento do capital fictício: a crise financeira internacional e suas consequências no Brasil. Departamento de Economia da Universidade de Brasília - UnB, texto No. 358, Brasília, Brasil.

Morningstar, 2016. Toyota Motor Corporation. Total Executive Compensation. Available at: http://insiders.morningstar.com/trading/executive-compensation. action?t=TM&region=usa&culture=en-US. Accessed 21 October 2016.

Nasdaq, 2015a. Ford Institutional Holdings. Available at: www.nasdaq.com/market-activity/stocks/f/institutional-holdings. Accessed 16 April 2016.

Nasdaq, 2015b. Largest stock acquisitions at General Motors. Available at: www.nasdaq.com/market-activity/stocks/gm/institutional-holdings. Accessed 19 February 2016.

Nasdaq, 2016a. State Street Corp. Available at: www.nasdaq.com/market-activity/institutional-portfolio/state-street-corp-6697. Accessed 21 November 2016.

Nasdaq, 2016b. GM Institutional Holdings. Available at: www.nasdaq.com/market-activity/stocks/gm/institutional-holdings. Accessed 19 February 2016.

Nasdaq, 2016c. Ford's New Institutional Holders. Available at: www.nasdaq.com/market-activity/stocks/f/institutional-holdings. Accessed 30 December 2016.

Nasdaq, 2016d. Ford Dividend History. Available at: www.nasdaq.com/market-activity/stocks/f/dividend-history. Accessed 20 May 2021.

Nasdaq, 2016e. Ford Financials. Available at: www.nasdaq.com/market-activity/stocks/f/financials. Accessed 20 May 2021.

Nasdaq, 2016f. GM Revenue EPS. Available at: www.nasdaq.com/market-activity/stocks/gm/revenue-eps. Accessed 20 May 2021.

Nasdaq, 2016g. GM Financials. Available at: www.nasdaq.com/market-activity/stocks/gm/financials. Accessed 20 May 2021.

Nasdaq, 2016h. Toyota Motor Corporation Financials. Available at: www.nasdaq.com/market-activity/stocks/tm/financials. Accessed 20 May 2021.

Nasdaq, 2018. BlackRock, Inc. Available at: www.nasdaq.com/market-activity/institutional-portfolio/blackrock-inc-711679. Accessed 21 April 2020.

Nasdaq, 2020a. Five Top-Performing Vanguard Funds of 2019. Available at: www.nasdaq.com/articles/5-top-performing-vanguard-funds-of-2019-2020-01-27. Accessed 3 November 2020.

Nasdaq, 2020b. Largest stock acquisitions at Ford. www.nasdaq.com/market-activity/stocks/f/institutional-holdings. Accessed 30 September 2020.

Nasdaq, 2020c. Largest stock acquisitions at Toyota – USA. Available at: www.nasdaq.com/market-activity/stocks/tm/institutional-holdings. Accessed 30 September 2020.

Nasdaq, 2020d. Toyota Motor Corporation Financials. Available at: www.nasdaq.com/market-activity/stocks/tm/financials. Accessed 20 May 2021.

Newberry, S. and Robb, A., 2008. Financialisation: constructing shareholder value...for some. *Critical Perspectives on Accounting*, 19, 5, pp. 741–763.

Noble, G. W., 2010. Fordism Light: Hyundai's challenge to coordinated capitalism. Institute of Social Science, University of Tokyo. *BRIE Working Paper* 186.

Payscale, 2015. Average Salary for Ford Motor Company Employees. Available at: www.payscale.com/research/US/Employer=Ford_Motor_Company/Salary. Accessed 21 May 2021.

Payscale, 2016. Average Salary for Volkswagen AG Employees. Available at: www.payscale.com/research/US/Employer=Volkswagen_ag/Salary. Accessed 30 March 2016.

Payscale, 2020. Average salary for General Motors Corporation Employees. Available at: www.payscale.com/research/US/Employer=General_Motors_Corporation/Salary. Accessed 20 December 2020.

Piketty, T., 2014. *O Capital no século XXI*. Editora Intrínseca, Rio de Janeiro.

Rappaport, A. 1981. Selecting strategies that create shareholder value. *Harvard Business Review*. Available at: https://hbr.org/1981/05/selecting-strategies-that-create-shareholder-value. Accessed 25 June 2016.

Rappaport, A. 2006. Ten ways to create shareholder value. *Harvard Business Review*, September 2006. Available at: https://hbr.org/2006/09/ten-ways-to-create-shareholder-value. Accessed 25 June 2016.

Reuters, 2014. Toyota gives Japan workers biggest pay rise in 21 years. Available at: www.reuters.com/article/japan-wages-toyota-motor-idUSL3N0M91ID20140312. Accessed 21 May 2016.

Salary Explorer, 2020. Factory and Manufacturing Average Salaries in Japan. Available at: www.salaryexplorer.com/salary-survey.php?loc=107&loctype=1&job=33&jobtype=1. Accessed 20 December 2020.

Saltorato, P., Domingues, L. C., Donadone, J. C. and Guimarães, M. R. N., 2014. From Stores to Banks. The Financialization of the retail trade in Brazil. *Latin American Perspectives*. 198, 41, 5, pp. 110–128.

Serfati, C., 1999. O papel ativo dos grupos predominantemente industriais na financeirização da economia. *A mundialização financeira: gênese, custos e riscos*. Coordenado por François Chesnais, São Paulo: Editora Xamã.

Shimizu, K., 2015. The change in the wage system and its impact on the production management at Toyota: the end of Ohnoism? 23rd International

Colloquium of GERPISA International Network, 9–12 June 2015, EHESS Cachan, Paris.

Srivastava, R.K., Shervani, T.A. and Fahey, L. 1998. Market-based assets and shareholder value: a framework for analysis. *Journal of Marketing*, 62, pp. 2–18.

Statista, 2020. Median household income in the United States in 2019, by race or ethnic group. Available at: www.statista.com/statistics/233324/median-household-income-in-the-united-states-by-race-or-ethnic-group/. Accessed 20 January 2021.

Stout, L., 2013. *The Shareholder Value Myth*. Cornell Law Faculty Publications, Paper 771.

Toyota Motor Corporation, 2006–2018. Annual Reports. Available at: https://global.toyota/en/ir/library/annual/archives/. Accessed 24 May 2021.

Toyota Motor Corporation, 2014. Annual Report. Available at: www.toyota-global.com/pages/contents/investors/ir_library/annual/pdf/2014/ar14_e.pdf. Accessed 19 May 2021.

Toyota Motor Corporation, 2016a. Largest stock acquisitions at Toyota. Available at: www.toyota-global.com/investors/stock_information_ratings/outline.html. Accessed 19 September 2016.

Toyota Motor Corporation, 2016b. Board of Directors. Available at: https://global.toyota/en/company/profile/executives/2016.html. Accessed 1 April 2016.

Useem, M., 1996. *Investor Capitalism. How money managers are changing the face of Corporate America.* BasicBooks, New York.

US Inflation Calculator, 2016. Available at: www.usinflationcalculator.com/inflation/historical-inflation-rates/. Accessed 28 April 2016.

Van Der Zwan, N. 2014. Making sense of financialization. *Socio-Economic Review*, 12, pp. 99–129.

Vanguard Group, Inc., 2020. Fast facts about Vanguard. Available at: https://about.vanguard.com/who-we-are/fast-facts/. Accessed 4 December 2020.

Volkswagen AG, 2000. Annual Report. Available at: www.volkswagenag.com/presence/konzern/images/teaser/history/chronik/annual-report/2000-Annual-Report.pdf. Accessed 24 May 2021.

Volkswagen AG, 2001. Annual Report. Available at: www.volkswagenag.com/presence/konzern/images/teaser/history/chronik/annual-report/2001-Annual-Report.pdf. Accessed 24 May 2021.

Volkswagen AG, 2002. Annual Report. Available at: www.volkswagenag.com/presence/konzern/images/teaser/history/chronik/annual-report/2002-Annual-Report.pdf. Accessed 24 May 2021.

Volkswagen AG, 2003. Annual Report. Available at: www.volkswagenag.com/presence/konzern/images/teaser/history/chronik/annual-report/2003-Annual-Report.pdf. Accessed 24 May 2021.

Volkswagen AG, 2004. Annual Report. Available at: www.volkswagenag.com/presence/konzern/images/teaser/history/chronik/annual-report/2004-Annual-Report.pdf. Accessed 24 May 2021.

Volkswagen AG, 2005. Annual Report. Available at: www.volkswagenag. com/presence/konzern/images/teaser/history/chronik/annual-report/2005-Annual-Report.pdf. Accessed 24 May 2021.

Volkswagen AG, 2006. Annual Report. Available at: www.volkswagenag. com/presence/konzern/images/teaser/history/chronik/annual-report/2006-Annual-Report.pdf. Accessed 24 May 2021.

Volkswagen AG, 2007. Annual Report. Available at: www.volkswagenag. com/presence/konzern/images/teaser/history/chronik/annual-report/2007-Annual-Report.pdf. Accessed 24 May2021.

Volkswagen AG, 2008–2020. Annual Reports. Available at: www.volkswagenag. com/en/InvestorRelations/news-and-publications/Annual_Reports.html. Accessed 20 May 2021.

Volkswagen AG, 2012. Annual Report 2012. Available at: www.volkswagenag. com/presence/konzern/images/teaser/history/chronik/annual-report/2012-Annual-Report.pdf. Accessed 20 May 2021.

Volkswagen AG, 2014. Annual Report 2014. Available at: https:// annualreport2014.volkswagenag.com/consolidated-financial-statements/ statement-of-comprehensive-income.html. Accessed 20 May 2021.

Volkswagen AG, 2015a. Annual Report 2015. Available at: https:// annualreport2015. volkswagenag.com/consolidated-financial-statements. html. Accessed 15 February 2017.

Volkswagen AG, 2015b. Shareholder Structure. Available at: www.volkswagenag. com/en/InvestorRelations/shares/shareholder-structure.html. Accessed 30 December 2015.

Volkswagen AG, 2016. Members of the Board of Management and their appointments. Available at: https://annualreport2016.volkswagenag.com/ group-management-report/executive-bodies/board-of-management.html. Accessed 31 December 2016.

Wartzman, R., 2017. *The End of Loyalty: The Rise and Fall of Good Jobs in America.* Public Affairs, New York.

Webber, David H., 2018. *The Rise of the Working-Class Shareholder: Labor's Last Best Weapon.* Harvard University Press, Cambridge, MA.

Willis Towers Watson, 2019. The world's largest 500 asset managers. Thinking Ahead Institute and Pensions & Investments joint research. Available at: www.thinkingaheadinstitute.org/research-papers/the-worlds-largest-asset-managers-2020/. Accessed 12 January 2021.

Woomack, J. P., Jones, D. T. and Roos, D., 2004. *A máquina que mudou o mundo.* 10ª edição, Elsevier.

Yahoo Finance, 2016a. Ford's Top Mutual Funds Holder. Available at: https:// finance.yahoo.com/quote/f/holders?ltr=1&guccounter=1. Accessed 14 September 2016.

Yahoo Finance, 2016b. General Motors' Top Mutual Fund Holders. Available at: https://finance.yahoo.com/quote/GM/holders?ltr=1. Accessed 14 September 2016.

Yoon, J. S., 2020. Average annual wage in South Korea 2000–2019. Available at: www.statista.com/statistics/557759/south-korea-average-annual-wage/#:~: text=In%202019%2C%20the%20average%20annual,purchasing%20 power%20parity%20(PPP). Accessed 16 November 2020.

Zilbovicius, M and Dias, A. V. C., 2006. A produção face à financeirização: quais as consequências para a organização da produção e do trabalho? Uma proposta de agenda de pesquisa para a Engenharia de Produção brasileira. In: XXVI ENEGEP– Fortaleza, CE, Brasil, 9 a 11 de outubro.

Zilbovicius, M and Marx, R., 2011. What is the role for Brazil in the new automotive industry? Threats and opportunities in a changing future for the car and its industry. Gerpisa colloquium, Paris.

Index

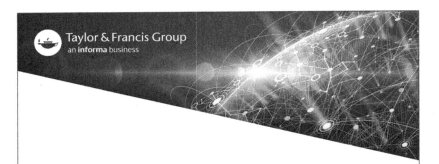

Printed in the United States
by Baker & Taylor Publisher Services